More Savoring God

More Savoring God

Praying with All Our Senses

Kathleen Finley

RESOURCE *Publications* • Eugene, Oregon

MORE SAVORING GOD
Praying with All Our Senses

Copyright © 2012 Kathleen Finley. All rights reserved. Except for brief quotations in critical publications or reviews, no part of this book may be reproduced in any manner without prior written permission from the publisher. Write: Permissions, Wipf and Stock Publishers, 199 W. 8th Ave., Suite 3, Eugene, OR 97401.

Resource Publications
An Imprint of Wipf and Stock Publishers
199 W. 8th Ave., Suite 3
Eugene, OR 97401

www.wipfandstock.com

ISBN 13: 978-1-61097-937-5

Scripture quotations, unless otherwise noted, are from the New Revised Standard Version Bible: Catholic Edition, copyright 1989, 1993, Division of Christian Education of the National Council of the Churches of Christ in the United States of America. Used by permission. All rights reserved.
Introduction used by permission of Ave Maria Press.

Made in the U.S.A.

This book is for my three sons,
Sean, Patrick, and Kevin,
who have taught me much about prayer
just by being who they are

Contents

Introduction: Our Senses Are There For a Reason ix

In the Office and at School

1. Candle: The Light of Christ 3
2. Clock and Calendar: Now Is the Acceptable Time 6
3. Bills: What Credit Is That to You? 12
4. Marker or Crayon: God's Gentle Mercy 17
5. Voice: You Know Mine 22
6. Photograph: In God's Image 27
7. Book: In the Book of Life 32
8. Map or Globe: Where Can I Go? 37
9. Letters of the Alphabet: I Am the Alpha and the Omega 43
10. Flag or Symbol: More Than Meets the Eye 47
11. Eraser: Wipe Away My Offenses 52

Around the House

12. Ruler: A Generous Measure 59
13. Cup or Mug: Let It Pass from Me 63
14. Door: I Stand and Knock 67
15. Towel and Soap: Create in Me a Clean Heart 72
16. Pills or Medicine: The Gift of Health 77
17. Newspaper: Believe in the Good News 82
18. Clothing: Put On Love 86
19. Hammer and Nails: A Time to Build 91
20. Bandage: You Have Healed Me 96
21. Needle and Thread: A Time to Sew 100

Contents

All Around Us

- 22 A Leaf or Branch: Alive in Christ 107
- 23 Ribbon or Bow: Gifts from God 110
- 24 A Feather or Egg: Consider the Birds of the Air 114
- 25 Music: Make a Joyful Noise 117
- 26 Moon and Stars: Look Up and See 122
- 27 Window: Let Me See Your Love 127
- 28 Basket: Woven In Love 131
- 29 Seashell: Like the Sands of the Sea 136
- 30 Name: I Have Called You 141
- 31 Favorite Smell: A Pleasing Fragrance 146

For Further Reading 151

Introduction: Our Senses Are There For a Reason

FASTEN YOUR SPIRITUAL SEAT belt. This book is an invitation to a different way of praying—and to a different way of seeing. (For those readers who have already discovered the earlier companion book, *Savoring God: Praying With All Our Senses*, you're in for a further treat.)

Usually when we pray we try to shut out the outside world and focus on the interior, the spiritual, the realm that we often think of as beyond or above us—the transcendent—in order to be able to be with God. Instead, this book invites you to be with God *through* the very tangible, specific objects of your everyday life, to take another look—as well as another listen, taste, touch and smell—at what is right before you and to see God there. God has given us our five senses as important ways to understand and appreciate the world around us; this is an opportunity to use them specifically for prayer.

The Hebrew and Christian scriptures remind us that in Jesus our God is a God-with-us, Emmanuel. Christians believe that Jesus was, and is, God incarnate or, as a wonderful young theologian-to-be put it, "God's show-and-tell." In Jesus *all* of human life and creation has become a sign of God's presence, filled with sacraments with a small "s," with ways to grow closer to God if we just look again—re-spect—what is right before us.

Jesus was very aware of our senses and spent much of his ministry healing the senses of those who came to him. When John the Baptist sent some of his followers to ask Jesus whether he was the Messiah, the Chosen One, listen to his response to them: "Go and tell John what you have seen and heard: the blind receive their sight, the lame walk, the lepers are cleansed, the deaf hear, the dead are raised, the poor have good news brought to them" [Luke 7:22]. We see scene after scene in the gospels

Introduction

where Jesus is healing those who are blind and deaf—and as we hear this Good News, each of us, in turn, is invited to see and hear more fully.

However, we're realizing that different people may see and hear in many different ways. We've learned a lot in the past century about different personality types and different learning styles. Whether it's the sixteen Myers-Briggs personality types based on Carl Jung's work or the nine Enneagram numbers or an awareness of the primary ways or styles through which we learn, we are coming to a deeper realization that we don't all do things the same way. This includes praying; in the words of the title of a helpful book by Dr. Charles Keating, *Who We Are Is How We Pray*.

If you see yourself as a hands-on person and learner—someone with what the experts call bodily-kinesthetic intelligence—or someone who has a hard time focusing on a fold-your-hands-and-close-your-eyes type of prayer without becoming distracted, this approach may be for you. However, it's not for everyone.

This is an experiment—or, more properly, a series of experiments—in a different, perhaps more playful, imaginative and right-brained approach to prayer than you may be used to. It may seem silly at times—who ever heard of praying with keys or underwear? See if this works for you. If it doesn't, keep looking; you'll find a way of prayer that will work well for you. God is eager to "get through" to each one of us and gives us an incredible variety of gifts every day—from sunsets to thunderstorms—to get our attention and to remind us of our Creator's limitless love for each of us.

In our relationship with this gracious God, prayer is a time for us to slow down a bit, focus ourselves and be with God, to spend time with the Creator as we would with a good friend. To put it informally, prayer is time to "hang out" with God. But often good quality "hanging out"—whether with a friend or with God—may take a bit of planning and clearing the schedule to help it happen. Probably the most difficult part of this—or any—type of prayer is finding a place and a time for that prayer, so that the rest of life doesn't just take over and monopolize all one's time and energy with busyness.

Plan for 10 to 15 minutes as you begin these prayer exercises; you may want to spend more time later as you get into it. It's good to have a space where you won't be disturbed for that amount of time, whether that means shutting the door to the room where you are, letting the answering machine handle any phone calls or even putting up a "do not disturb" sign.

Introduction

If that's not possible, maybe you can grab a cup of coffee at the kitchen table while the kids are playing in the other room. It sounds hard to do, but you're worth it! Think of it as finding a quiet space to have a catch-up long-distance call with someone you haven't talked to in a while! (But faith tells us that it's really not that long a distance at all to God!)

There is no particular order to these suggested prayer exercises, except that it's helpful to start with the one using a candle, because we will then use the candle as a focus point in the other exercises. ("Exercises" seems to be the best term for these prayers, since calling them "meditations" seems too formal, and in a way they are like exercises you might do to help increase the strength of your eyesight or hearing or another of the senses.)

After making sure you have on hand what is needed for the particular exercise, sit comfortably—but not *too comfortably*—take a few deep breaths, light the candle as instructed, and begin. (If you don't have a particular object called for in one of the exercises, substitute something that would work for you or skip that particular exercise.) There are several parts to each of these exercises.

The first section is *Centering*, with a suggested prayer to help you recover a sense of God's presence, a presence which we know is always with us but one which we can forget so much of the time. This is the time to prepare ourselves to just "be" with God. Try spreading your hands open during the opening prayer so that you use your body even here. If the written prayer is not helpful to you and you would rather use your own words or a different prayer, please use what works for you.

The second section is *Savoring*, a time to use your senses to explore the particular object in the prayer exercise. When you are touching or looking or using your other senses in the prayer exercise, try to do it as if for the very first time, hungrily, the way an infant or toddler seems to take in information; God wants to come to you through your senses.

Next comes *Listening*, a chance to explore how God's word is connected to this particular object or image and to deepen your perception of the object in light of the Christian tradition. There are several scripture passages given; you may wish to focus on just one of them or to read and savor each one. It is important not to hurry here but to roll God's word here around in your head and let it mix with what you're seeing before you and what your other senses have told you. Reading the passage aloud may help your ears to become involved as well as your eyes.

Introduction

Considering, which is a time to reflect on that object, comes next. This is a time to think about the ways that this object interacts with us in our daily lives, to take what we may know about this object and make the connections to our spirituality.

Last, but certainly not least, is the section called *Responding*. This is an opportunity to explore the implications of our reflection for the rest of our lives, the so-what factor. John Shea once commented that the result of prayer for the Christian is always new action. What difference will this prayer make in my life after I finish it? Is there anything that I will do or see in a new way as a result of this prayer time? This section suggests some possibilities; only you can decide what that might be in your own life. This section ends with a brief prayer and with the word "Amen," an ancient Hebrew word meaning "It is true."

If at all possible, after the prayer exercise it would be good to leave the object that you prayed with out in a prominent place for a few days as a reminder of your prayer and the need to stay open to God's goodness.

These exercises are just the beginning of what can happen in this approach to prayer; there are many more possibilities to pray with, based on each person's interests and the unique setting of every life. Gardeners, for example, will probably want to pray with some garden tools, teens with symbols of their lives, and those with babies with a diaper and the infant toys that are so much a part of their lives. Those involved with a particular sport can pray with symbols of that sport, and musicians can pray with their instruments, while those with disabilities will want to pray with a symbol of that challenge in their lives. The possibilities are nearly endless.

These exercises can also be used well with a group; be sure to use enough time for each person in the group to consider the object or objects being prayed with.

Hopefully, the result of this kind of prayer for you will be a new way of beginning to taste and see God's presence (or presents) all around you. Blessings to you on your journey of discovery!

O taste and see that the LORD is good. [Ps 34:8]

In the Office and at School

CHAPTER 1

Candle: The Light of Christ

MATERIALS AT HAND: A favorite candle, scented or unscented, and a match or lighter for it. If possible, do this in a darkened or dimly lit area.

CENTERING (With hands spread open, say:)

Loving God, Creator of all that is,
here I am—today, in this place,
with all the senses you have given me.
Help me to use them to experience you more deeply.
You are present everywhere around me;
open me to know more of the many ways
that your goodness surrounds me.
Thank you for this time to be with you and to listen to you.
Amen.

SAVORING (Senses at Work):

Look at the unlit candle as it waits to do what it was meant to do: give light. Touch it and sense its texture and shape. Smell it to determine if it has a scent or not.

Now prepare to light it and watch as the candle is slowly transformed into a source of light. Smell the bit of smoke as the wick lights and as the match is blown out, if you are using a match. If we were to use this candle or the source of its flame to light many candles, the light of this one would not be diminished in any way. This light could be magnified many times without diminishing any of the flames it helped "foster."

Hold your hands close enough to the flame to feel the warmth without being burned and watch how the candle's light changes the appearance of the objects around it as it throws the light that is and is not its own.

LISTENING (The Word of God):

Listen to one or more of these passages as you watch the candle's flame:

Again Jesus spoke to them, saying, "I am the light of the world. Whoever follows me will never walk in darkness but will have the light of life." [John 8:12]

It is you who light my lamp; the LORD, my God, lights up my darkness. [Ps 18:28]

The LORD is my light and my salvation; whom shall I fear? The LORD is the stronghold of my life; of whom shall I be afraid? [Ps 27:1]

"You are the light of the world. A city built on a hill cannot be hid. No one after lighting a lamp puts it under the bushel basket, but on the lampstand, and it gives light to all in the house. In the same way, let your light shine before others, so that they may see your good works and give glory to your Father in heaven. [Matt 5:14–16]

CONSIDERING (Time to Reflect):

Until the last century or so, our only source of light was candles and lamps of various sorts, apart from sunlight. Although we don't often experience total darkness in our culture, the symbol of light as truth in the midst of the darkness of falsity and fear and evil is still a strong and powerful one.

Our God is the ultimate source of light and truth; St. Paul, for example, experienced Christ's presence at the time of his conversion as a strong light which asked Paul why he was persecuting Christ in the early Christians. This light blinded Paul until he could fully "see" in faith.

Candle: The Light of Christ

Loving God, help me to "see" more clearly how You are the light in my life and to appreciate the ways that You dispel the darkness of my doubts and fears with the strong flame of Your love.

RESPONDING (So what?):

In the first Letter of John we read. "Whoever says, 'I am in the light,' while hating a brother or sister, is still in the darkness. Whoever loves a brother or sister lives in the light, and in such a person there is no cause for stumbling." [1 John 2:9–10]

If I am to really live in the light, then I need to realize that God's love and light is there for *everyone* around me, even the person I find it hardest to love right now. (Name a specific person or two for yourself here.)

Loving God and source of all light, help me to bring the light of Your love to all whom I meet and work with. Amen.

(We will be using the candle in the other meditations to help us focus on God's presence.)

CHAPTER 2

Clock and Calendar: Now Is the Acceptable Time

MATERIALS AT HAND. A clock or watch and a calendar, with a candle as a prayer focus.

CENTERING: (Light the candle and say with your hands spread open:)

Loving God, Creator of all that is,
here I am—today, in this place,
with all the senses you have given me.
Help me to use them to experience you more deeply.
You are present everywhere around me;
open me to know more of the many ways
that your goodness surrounds me.
Thank you for this time to be with you and to listen to You.
Amen.

SAVORING:

Look at the watch or clock and the calendar before you, pretending for a moment that you have never seen either one before in your life. What a wonderful and helpful idea, you might think, to be able to keep track of the minutes and hours, the days, months and years that go by and to plan for the future. It is easy indeed to take these helpful tools for granted.

Clock and Calendar: Now Is the Acceptable Time

Hold the calendar in your hands. Does each of its pages record a day, a week, a month or does it show the whole year on a page? Which do you prefer and why? Look back through the calendar pages that mark the part of the year that has already passed—if they are still attached—touching as you do the place where the days that have passed are recorded and thanking God for the gift of that time in your life. Then move on to the pages marking the time yet to come this year, touching them and asking God to be with you and to bless that time in the future. What's your favorite day or time of year? Why?

Now hold the watch or clock. Does it make any noise? Listen to see. How important is it to you to know exactly what time it is and to be on time? Do you remember learning to tell time? Do you prefer an analog clock (or watch) that has hands or a digital one that displays the current time in numbers? Why? What's the best time of the day for you and why? Are you more of a morning person or a night person, and how do you know? Have you experienced a period of time when you didn't know what time it was? How was that for you?

What a faithful job this time-telling device does for you, telling you whenever you care to look its way what the time is where you live. What do you think might be happening in your life if you lived in a time zone several hours ahead or even twelve hours different from where you live? Have you ever had to cope with much of a time difference when traveling?

Whether we consider our days, weeks and months or seconds, minutes and hours, time is truly a precious gift from God.

LISTENING:

Listen to one or more of these passages as you watch the candle play across the calendar and clock or watch:

And God said, "Let there be lights in the dome of the sky to separate the day from the night; and let them be for signs and for seasons and for days and years, and let them be lights in the dome of the sky to give light upon the earth." And it was so. (Gen 1:14–15)

. . . teach us to count our days that we may gain a wise heart. (Ps 90:12)

In the Home and at School

For everything there is a season, and a time for every matter under heaven: a time to be born, and a time to die; a time to plant, and a time to pluck up what is planted; a time to kill, and a time to heal; a time to break down, and a time to build up; a time to weep, and a time to laugh; a time to mourn, and a time to dance; a time to throw away stones, and a time to gather stones together; a time to embrace, and a time to refrain from embracing; a time to seek, and a time to lose; a time to keep, and a time to throw away; a time to tear, and a time to sew; a time to keep silence, and a time to speak; a time to love, and a time to hate; a time for war, and a time for peace . . . [God] has made everything suitable for its time; moreover he has put a sense of past and future into [people's] minds, yet they cannot find out what God has done from the beginning to the end. (Eccl 3:1–8,11)

Bless the Lord, nights and days; sing praise to him and highly exalt him forever. (Dan 3:71)

Why is one day more important than another, when all the daylight in the year is from the sun. By the Lord's wisdom they were distinguished, and he appointed the different seasons and festivals. Some days he exalted and hallowed, and some he made ordinary days. (Sir 33:7–9])

Now after John was arrested, Jesus came to Galilee, proclaiming the good news of God, and saying, "The time is fulfilled, and the kingdom of God has come near; repent, and believe in the good news." (Mark 1:14–15)

And can any of you by worrying add a single hour to your span of life? . . . Therefore do not worry, saying, 'What will we eat?' or 'What will we drink?' or 'What will we wear? For it is the Gentiles who strive for all these things; and indeed your heavenly Father knows that you need all these things. But strive first for the kingdom of God and his righteousness, and all these things will be given to you as well. So do not worry about tomorrow, for tomorrow will bring worries of its own. Today's trouble is enough for today. (Matt 6:27,31–34)

CONSIDERING:

Both the calendar and the clock that lie before you are the fruits of many attempts to try to measure time, with varying degrees of accuracy.

Clock and Calendar: Now Is the Acceptable Time

We know that each day is based on how long it takes the earth to rotate once on its axis and that each year is based on how long it takes the earth to move once around the sun. But it takes our planet 365 days, 5 hours, 48 minutes and 45.5 seconds to rotate around the sun, an amount of time difficult to divide up evenly.

And months are also difficult to calculate. Originally, months were based on the length from one full moon to the next, which is only 29 1/2 days. Twelve of these lunar months were 11 1/4 days short of a solar year, so that an extra month had to be added every couple years to keep the seasons consistent. (The seven-day week, by the way, doesn't come from a clear source in nature; its origins are in the Jewish tradition of a sabbath day of rest after six days of work.)

Our modern western calendar, with its irregular months and a leap year every four years actually owes a great deal to the Roman emperor Julius Caesar who, in 45 BC, helped set up most of the structures and names we use today. We even have a month named for him—July—and one for his successor, Augustus. In 325 Pope Gregory XIII helped fine tune the Julian calendar because ten extra days had accumulated as the result of a miscalculation.

This Gregorian calendar is still in use today in most of the world; it is mainly a Christian calendar, counting years from the birth of Christ. There are also Jewish and Islamic calendars, both of which are based largely on the lunar month, as well as many other kinds of calendars throughout history. Various current proposals for a reform to the calendar, with more uniform months and weeks, have not so far been successful.

Clocks have also had an interesting evolution. Shadow clocks and sundials were some of the earliest ways of keeping track of time in ancient times, which made the task far more challenging on a cloudy day. Through the centuries, people have used marked candles, knotted ropes, water, and hourglasses to help mark the time. Later, clocks were first powered by bulky mechanical works, then pendulums and springs and now electric, battery or even atomic energy. As the technology has improved, so did the accuracy, as well as sometimes the price and the flexibility in size of the timepiece.

It has indeed taken us humans a long while to figure out how to measure and understand this gift of time.

In the Home and at School

RESPONDING:

We know that each of us only has a limited amount of days in our lives. Psalm 139 reminds us that God is the only one who knows how long that will be:

O LORD, you have searched me and known me.... For it was you who formed my inward parts; you knit me together in my mother's womb.... Your eyes beheld my unformed substance. In your book were written all the days that were formed for me, when none of them as yet existed. (Ps 139:1,13,16)

Perhaps because of all our clocks and calendars we can tend to think that we each have all the "time" in the world, when we really know that's not true. Scripture often reminds us that the time is now for us to look at what's really important in our lives and act with that in mind. For example, St. Paul reminds the Christians in Corinth:

As we work together with [Christ], we urge you also not to accept the grace of God in vain. For [God] says, "At an acceptable time I have listened to you, and on a day of salvation I have helped you." See, now is the acceptable time; see, now is the day of salvation! (2 Cor 6:1–2)

And the book of Sirach also nudges us. "Do not delay to turn back to the Lord, and do not postpone it from day to day; for suddenly the wrath of the Lord will come upon you, and at the time of punishment you will perish." (Sir 5:7)

If you knew that your "time" was short in this life, is there anything that would you change about your life? What regrets would you have? Would you spend more time just enjoying life and not working so hard? Would you spend more time with your family and friends? Travel more? Or what?

Spiritual masters tell us that to live with the reality of death every day of our lives is not as morbid as it seems; it can help us see life with a clearer perspective. Think of a couple specific ways that you might live differently if you knew you had perhaps a month to live. Then resolve to live that way in the next week or two and see whether your life seems any different.

God of my days and nights, my minutes and hours, my months and years, thank you for every bit of the time you have given me in my life. Help me to use it wisely. Bless those who make and sell—and at times, repair—our clocks and watches, calendars and all the ways we keep track

Clock and Calendar: Now Is the Acceptable Time

of our time. Bless my family and friends and all those whose birthdays and anniversaries, trips and gatherings fill my calendar. Bless especially those who are coming near to the end of their lives; be with them in a special way to comfort them.

Please help me appreciate the gift of your time in my life in a new way every time I see a clock or calendar. Amen.

(You may want to celebrate the gift of time, as some families do, with a blessing of clocks and calendars every New Year's Eve or New Year's Day.)

CHAPTER 3

Bills: What Credit Is That To You?

Materials at hand. A few bills or sales slips or perhaps a tax statement and a credit card or two, with a candle as a prayer focus.

CENTERING (Light the candle and say with your hands spread open:)

Loving God, Creator of all that is,
here I am—today, in this place,
with all the senses you have given me.
Help me to use them to experience you more deeply.
You are present everywhere around me;
open me to know more of the many ways
that your goodness surrounds me.
Thank you for this time to be with you and to listen to you.
Amen.

SAVORING:

Look at the bills (and the credit card or cards) before you. Remind yourself that this is a time to *pray with* these reminders of our transactions, not to worry about them, which is often what we're used to doing.

These pieces of paper (and plastic) before you with their names and numbers, with corporate logos and addresses, are all that remain of transactions and services, ways that others have helped you—or could help you, in the case of insurance—or ways that you help pay your part in the community in which you live, in the case of utility bills and taxes.

Bills: What Credit Is That To You?

These pieces of paper have been answered, or will be, with other pieces of paper: checks or paper money or, at times today, their electronic equivalent. These responses acknowledge how much we rely on others' help in the world in which we live. In fact, our lives are full of interactions in which we are "indebted" to others for all that they do for us.

LISTENING:

Listen to one or more of these passages as you watch the candle play across the bills and credit card(s):

Do to others as you would have them do to you. If you love those who love you, what credit is that to you? For even sinners love those who love them. If you do good to those who do good to you, what credit is that to you? For even sinners do the same. If you lend to those from whom you hope to receive, what credit is that to you? Even sinners lend to sinners, to receive as much again. But love your enemies, do good, and lend, expecting nothing in return. Your reward will be great, and you will be children of the Most High; for he is kind to the ungrateful and the wicked. Be merciful, just as your Father is merciful. (Luke 6:31–36)

Pay to all what is due them—taxes to whom taxes are due, revenue to whom revenue is due, respect to whom respect is due, honor to whom honor is due. Owe no one anything, except to love one another; for the one who loves another has fulfilled the law. (Rom 13:7–8)

Then Peter came and said to him, "Lord, if another member of the church sins against me, how often should I forgive? As many as seven times? Jesus said to him, "Not seven times, but, I tell you, seventy-seven times. (Matt 18:21–35)

Even tax collectors came to be baptized, and they asked [John the Baptist], "Teacher, what should we do?. He said to them, "Collect no more than the amount prescribed for you." (Luke 3:12–13)

One of the Pharisees asked Jesus to eat with him, and he went into the Pharisee's house and took his place at the table. And a woman in the city, who was a sinner, having learned that he was eating in the Pharisee's house, brought an alabaster jar of ointment. She stood behind him at his feet, weeping, and began to bathe his feet with her tears and to dry them

In the Home and at School

with her hair. Then she continued kissing his feet and anointing them with the ointment. Now when the Pharisee who had invited him saw it, he said to himself, "If this man were a prophet, he would have known who and what kind of woman this is who is touching him—that she is a sinner. Jesus spoke up and said to him, "Simon, I have something to say to you." "Teacher," he replied, "speak. "A certain creditor had two debtors; one owed five hundred denarii, and the other fifty. When they could not pay, he canceled the debts for both of them. Now which of them will love him more? Simon answered, "I suppose the one for whom he canceled the greater debt." And Jesus said to him, "You have judged rightly.. Then turning toward the woman, he said to Simon, "Do you see this woman? I entered your house; you gave me no water for my feet, but she has bathed my feet with her tears and dried them with her hair. You gave me no kiss, but from the time I came in she has not stopped kissing my feet. You did not anoint my head with oil, but she has anointed my feet with ointment. Therefore, I tell you, her sins, which were many, have been forgiven; hence she has shown great love. But the one to whom little is forgiven, loves little." (Luke 7:36–47)

When you make your neighbor a loan of any kind, you shall not go into the house to take the pledge. You shall wait outside, while the person to whom you are making the loan brings the pledge out to you. If the person is poor, you shall not sleep in the garment given you as the pledge. You shall give the pledge back by sunset, so that your neighbor may sleep in the cloak and bless you; and it will be to your credit before the LORD your God. (Deut 24:10–13)

He called the crowd with his disciples, and said to them, "If any want to become my followers, let them deny themselves and take up their cross and follow me. For those who want to save their life will lose it, and those who lose their life for my sake, and for the sake of the gospel, will save it. For what will it profit them to gain the whole world and forfeit their life. Indeed, what can they give in return for their life? (Mark 8:34–37)

CONSIDERING:

Most of the bills we have and pay are a result of the establishment of credit, a process that goes back to the Middle Ages when, as wealth became greater, people often got tired of carrying all their gold around and would leave it with the goldsmith until they needed it. The goldsmiths quickly realized that they had an amount of money on hand that their clients didn't need immediately that they could lend out in the meantime, with a promissory note for the principal amount and some interest. Such money-lending practices made prominent banking families of the time, like the Medicis, quite wealthy.

Eventually, the notes themselves often were circulated as currency instead of the gold they represented. And the rest, as they say, is history. Paper money and credit and lending has been indispensable to the development of the modern world ever since.

One of the kinds of "bills" we have to pay, either directly or indirectly, is that of taxes. Often in history taxes were paid in kind, by labor or other goods rather than money. But in contemporary society, the government seems to want our money to be able to support its services to all the citizens.

The problem with taxation in the Judea of Jesus' time was that the Jews who collected taxes for the Romans were hated for cooperating with the enemy—and they also usually ended up keeping a percentage for themselves. Nonetheless, we are told that Jesus often spent time with tax collectors and sinners, the outcasts of his society. Jesus knew that all of us—from the least to the greatest—"owe" our biggest "debt" to God: our very existence, a "bill" that we can never fully "repay."

RESPONDING:

Paying our bills and taxes provide us with some "interest"-ing images on which to reflect. For example, when the Pharisees had tried to trap Jesus by asking him whether it was legal to pay taxes to the Roman emperor, Jesus once again outsmarted them by asking for a coin and inquiring as to whose head was on it. When they answered that it was the emperor's, he said to them, "Give therefore to the emperor the things that are the emperor's, and to God the things that are God's." (Matt 22:15–21)

An important question, therefore, for me to consider is, To whom do I owe what? I certainly owe my parents gratitude for helping me to become who I am, as well as my friends and others in my life. But God has given me my very life itself and the gift of every moment that I exist. What is my "credit rating" with God? Have I shown how grateful I am by the way in which I in turn love others? Is my "bottom line" one of forgiveness toward others like the forgiveness God continues to show me?

A couple important qualities to consider when it comes to money and credit matters are generosity and honesty, as Sirach, the book of Proverbs and the gospel of Luke remind us.

In Sirach we read, "The merciful lend to their neighbors; by holding out a helping hand they keep the commandments. Lend to your neighbor in his time of need; repay your neighbor when a loan falls due. Keep your promise and be honest with him, and on every occasion you will find what you need." (Sir 29:1–3). And the book of Proverbs cautions, "Treasures gained by wickedness do not profit, but righteousness delivers from death." (Prov 10:2])

Listen to Jesus talking about how to deal with wealth and indebtedness in Luke's gospel—and notice the Pharisees' response:

"'Whoever is faithful in a very little is faithful also in much; and whoever is dishonest in a very little is dishonest also in much. If then you have not been faithful with the dishonest wealth, who will entrust to you the true riches? And if you have not been faithful with what belongs to another, who will give you what is your own? No slave can serve two masters; for a slave will either hate the one and love the other, or be devoted to the one and despise the other. You cannot serve God and wealth.' The Pharisees, who were lovers of money, heard all this, and they ridiculed him." (Luke 16:10–14)

Loving God, help me to be "faith-full" and generous when I deal with money, whether I owe it to someone or someone owes it to me.

God of all the transactions in our lives, credit and debit, please bless all those involved with the business of giving and receiving credit, from accountants and bookkeepers to all those who issue and use the credit cards that are a big part of our lives these days. Bless those who are in debt and those who work in credit bureaus and credit counseling to help them. Bless, too, those developing nations of the world whose debts to other countries are crippling them as they try to cope with the needs of their own growing population.

And when I see a bill or a credit card, help me to remember that it is to You that I "owe" all that I am and the very gift of life itself. Amen.

CHAPTER 4

Marker or Crayon: God's Gentle Mercy

Materials at hand: A candle as a prayer focus, a marker or crayon (or both) and something to write on.

CENTERING (Light the candle and say with your hands spread open):

Loving God, Creator of all that is,
here I am—today, in this place,
with all the senses You have given me.
Help me to use them to experience You more deeply
You are present everywhere around me;
open me to know more of the many ways
that Your goodness surrounds me.
Thank you for this time to be with You and to listen to You.
Amen.

SAVORING:

Before you use the crayon or marker, take a look at how it is made without touching it yet. Notice details that you might usually miss as you quickly pick it up to use it. How is it shaped? What is the texture of the outside of it? Is the tip worn at all, if it's a crayon? How does the cap fit on it, if it is a marker? What color is it and what color does it mark when it does? What has it been used for, or what kind of uses may await it?

In the Home and at School

Now touch it with your eyes closed, so that your other senses are heightened. What does your sense of touch tell you? Are the textures what your eyes led you to believe? Is there any smell to the marker or crayon? If that involves taking off the cap, listen for any sound that may make as you do.

Now take the marker or crayon and make some random marks, much like a child might make, both with your eyes closed and then with them open, so that you can experience the action without seeing the result at first. Notice how it feels to leave some visible reminder behind of the action you have just performed.

This humble instrument is designed just to make a mark when and where that function is called for.

LISTENING:

Listen to one or more of these passages as you watch the candle play across the crayon or marker:

[W]en they were in the field, Cain rose up against his brother Abel, and killed him. Then the LORD said to Cain, "Where is your brother Abel?" He said, "I do not know; am I my brother's keeper? And the LORD said, "What have you done? Listen; your brother's blood is crying out to me from the ground. And now you are cursed from the ground, which has opened its mouth to receive your brother's blood from your hand. When you till the ground, it will no longer yield to you its strength; you will be a fugitive and a wanderer on the earth. Cain said to the LORD, "My punishment is greater than I can bear. Today you have driven me away from the soil, and I shall be hidden from your face; I shall be a fugitive and a wanderer on the earth, and anyone who meets me may kill me." Then the LORD said to him, "Not so! Whoever kills Cain will suffer a sevenfold vengeance." And the LORD put a mark on Cain, so that no one who came upon him would kill him. (Gen 4:8–15)

Out of the depths I cry to you, O LORD. Lord, hear my voice! Let your ears be attentive to the voice of my supplications. If you, O LORD, should mark iniquities, Lord, who could stand. But there is forgiveness with you, so that you may be revered. (Ps 130:1–4)

Marker or Crayon: God's Gentle Mercy

Then [the Lord] said to me, "Have you seen this, O mortal? Is it not bad enough that the house of Judah commits the abominations done here? Must they fill the land with violence, and provoke my anger still further?

. . . . Then he cried in my hearing with a loud voice, saying, "Draw near, you executioners of the city, each with his destroying weapon in his hand. And six men came from the direction of the upper gate, which faces north, each with his weapon for slaughter in his hand; among them was a man clothed in linen, with a writing case at his side. They went in and stood beside the bronze altar. Now the glory of the God of Israel had gone up from the cherub on which it rested to the threshold of the house. The LORD called to the man clothed in linen, who had the writing case at his side, and said to him, "Go through the city, through Jerusalem, and put a mark on the foreheads of those who sigh and groan over all the abominations that are committed in it. To the others he said in my hearing, "Pass through the city after him, and kill; your eye shall not spare, and you shall show no pity. Cut down old men, young men and young women, little children and women, but touch no one who has the mark. And begin at my sanctuary." (Ezekiel 8:17, 9:1–6)

There they crucified [Jesus], and with him two others, one on either side, with Jesus between them. Pilate . . . had an inscription written and put on the cross. It read, "Jesus of Nazareth, the King of the Jews. Many of the Jews read this inscription, because the place where Jesus was crucified was near the city; and it was written in Hebrew, in Latin, and in Greek.

Then the chief priests of the Jews said to Pilate, "Do not write, 'The King of the Jews,' but, 'This man said, I am King of the Jews.' Pilate answered, "What I have written I have written. (John 19:18–22)

Hear, O Israel: The LORD is our God, the LORD alone. You shall love the LORD your God with all your heart, and with all your soul, and with all your might. Keep these words that I am commanding you today in your heart.

Recite them to your children and talk about them when you are at home and when you are away, when you lie down and when you rise. Bind them as a sign on your hand, fix them as an emblem on your forehead and write them on the doorposts of your house and on your gates. (Deut 6:4–9)

In the Home and at School

CONSIDERING:

Through the centuries, humans have found many ways to mark what they needed to, from early marks that may have been carved into stone or wet clay, and later dried, to drawing or writing on walls of caves as early as 25,000 years ago with materials like charcoal and later early mixtures of found substances that were the earliest paints. While all peoples wish to leave a mark on the earth where they have been, the designs that have survived seem to have an especially important purpose for the community, even before the beginnings of modern alphabets and writing.

In our world today we have such a variety of tools for making designs, including every color imaginable and markers that are indelible as well as washable. We also have an increasing number of computer-assisted and technological means for rendering an accurate and polished image.

In scripture, marks are used in a variety of ways. We hear of the sign that Pontius Pilate had made for Jesus' cross, which detailed his claims and the charge against him so that no one would wonder what he had done. We also hear of the Israelites who, while they were slaves in Egypt were instructed to slay a goat for what would later become the Passover and to mark the doorway of their houses with the blood so that the angel of death would not strike anyone in that house. (Exodus 12) And we have the accounts of the mark of Cain and the vision of the prophet Ezekiel, both of whom experienced a mark as one of protection and of God's gentle and forgiving mercy, a love that always takes us back and one which we can never deserve or earn.

RESPONDING (So what?):

What kind of a "mark" have I made with my life? What will there be to show who and what I was after I am gone. Is there a word, a color, a design that could sum up my life so far?

Loving God of all, please bless all those who make and use markers and crayons, including children and artists, sign makers and graphic designers. Bless the students who may use them to highlight what they're studying and those who do not have these tools but could use them if they had them. Bless all those who vote, whether they use markers to "mark" their ballots or not; help them to use their ability to choose their leaders well.

Marker or Crayon: God's Gentle Mercy

And remind us of your "indelible" love for us, that marks us as your own and takes us back, even when we have pulled away from your love.
Amen.

CHAPTER 5

Voice: You Know Mine

MATERIALS AT HAND: A candle as a prayer focus, a recording of your voice on tape or on an answering machine or cell phone or just enough privacy to be able to speak aloud.

CENTERING (Light the candle and say—aloud if you can—with your hands spread open:)

Loving God, Creator of all that is,
here I am—today, in this place,
with all the senses you have given me.
Help me to use them to experience you more deeply.
You are present everywhere around me;
open me to know more of the many ways
that your goodness surrounds me.
Thank you for this time to be with you and to listen to you.
Amen.

SAVORING:

Take time to prepare your ears for hearing your own voice by predicting what you will sound like. Then, if you have a recorded source, turn it on and listen. Was it what you expected to hear? How was it different, if at all? Speech experts tell us that we are often surprised at the sound of our recorded voice- even not recognizing it at times- because when we hear ourselves, we hear in part through the bones in our head which, in effect, changes what we hear.

If you don't have a recorded source for your voice, listen as though you've never heard yourself before as you say something like, "This is my voice." Think for a moment of all the people who recognize that voice, most of whom are delighted to hear it when they do. Can you think of a time when you waited to hear the voice of someone you loved, wondering if they were safe after not having heard from them for a while, or a time when you heard a familiar voice when you had not expected to?

Are there any stories that you've been told about the process of your learning to talk? For example, did you have any favorite words or phrases as a child or any particular habits then, like stuttering or a lisp?

Speech is a power that is so easy to take for granted—until we have laryngitis or for some reason cannot use it, even temporarily.

LISTENING:

Listen to one or more of these passages as you watch the candle, perhaps playing across the tape recorder or answering machine, if you have used one:

But Moses said to the LORD, "O my Lord, I have never been eloquent, neither in the past nor even now that you have spoken to your servant; but I am slow of speech and slow of tongue." Then the LORD said to him, "Who gives speech to mortals? Who makes them mute or deaf, seeing or blind? Is it not I, the LORD? Now go, and I will be with your mouth and teach you what you are to speak." .... Then Moses went up to God; the LORD called to him from the mountain, saying, "Thus you shall say to the house of Jacob, and tell the Israelites: You have seen what I did to the Egyptians, and how I bore you on eagles' wings and brought you to myself. Now therefore, if you obey my voice and keep my covenant, you shall be my treasured possession out of all the peoples. (Exodus 4:10–12, 19:3–5)

The voice of the LORD is over the waters; the God of glory thunders, the LORD, over mighty waters. The voice of the LORD is powerful; the voice of the LORD is full of majesty. (Ps 29:3–4)

In the Home and at School

> When Zechariah saw [the angel] he was terrified; and fear overwhelmed him. But the angel said to him, "Do not be afraid, Zechariah, for your prayer has been heard. Your wife Elizabeth will bear you a son, and you will name him John. You will have joy and gladness, and many will rejoice at his birth, for he will be great in the sight of the Lord . . . . Zechariah said to the angel, "How will I know that this is so? For I am an old man, and my wife is getting on in years." The angel replied, "I am Gabriel. I stand in the presence of God, and I have been sent to speak to you and to bring you this good news. But now, because you did not believe my words, which will be fulfilled in their time, you will become mute, unable to speak, until the day these things occur." (Luke 1:12–15,18–20)

> The one who enters by the gate is the shepherd of the sheep. The gatekeeper opens the gate for him, and the sheep hear his voice. He calls his own sheep by name and leads them out. When he has brought out all his own, he goes ahead of them, and the sheep follow him because they know his voice. They will not follow a stranger, but they will run from him because they do not know the voice of strangers. (John 10:2–5)

> It was now about noon, and darkness came over the whole land until three in the afternoon, while the sun's light failed; and the curtain of the temple was torn in two. Then Jesus, crying with a loud voice, said, "Father, into your hands I commend my spirit." Having said this, he breathed his last. (Luke 23:44–46)

> Now as [Saul] was going along and approaching Damascus, suddenly a light from heaven flashed around him. He fell to the ground and heard a voice saying to him, "Saul, Saul, why do you persecute me?" He asked, "Who are you, Lord?" The reply came, "I am Jesus, whom you are persecuting. But get up and enter the city, and you will be told what you are to do." The men who were traveling with him stood speechless because they heard the voice but saw no one. (Acts 9:3–7)

CONSIDERING:

Human speech is still somewhat of a scientific mystery. Researchers know that it is formed by air passing through the vocal cords which cause various rates of vibration, but there are certain aspects of speech that continue to intrigue and puzzle those who study it.

Voice: You Know Mine

Our voices can vary in pitch, quality, and volume. Another variable is resonance, which has to do with our unique body structure and how our voice vibrates through our head and throat. Because of that variation, each of us produces a distinctive voiceprint, which is increasingly used for identification and security purposes. This spectographic picture of our spoken words is as unrepeatable as our fingerprints, the only one that will ever exist just like it. No one before or after you will have the exact voice that you do. When others hear your voice, they are receiving a sound that only you can make.

RESPONDING:

When I pray, how do I know that God really "hears" my unique voice? At times in scripture we read of people praying in a loud voice, as though God were so far away that one needed to shout to be heard, but in faith we know that God is as close as our very thoughts and always hears us. In fact, just as Jesus heard a voice at his baptism and at the Transfiguration saying, "You are my Son, the Beloved; with you I am well pleased." (Mark 1:11), so God's "voice" gives that same message to each of us: I am delighted with you just as you are. Loving God, help me to know how much you listen for, and delight in, my voice.

But how do I know that I am "listening to God's voice" in return, as I make choices in my life? In the Old Testament, listening to God's voice was made easier by the presence of the prophets, who were called to be the voice of God to their people, a kind of human tape recorder saying, "Thus says the Lord . . . ." However, too often the prophets found that people would not listen to their voice or to God's. As we try to understand God's "voice" in our lives, taking time for prayer and discernment– sometimes with the help of a spiritual director– can help us listen to the ways in which God is present.

The book of Sirach reminds us, "The flute and the harp make sweet melody, but a pleasant voice is better than either." (40:21) And the letter of James talks about the importance of how we speak to and about others by comparing the tongue to a horses bridle or the rudder of a ship, something small but with a lot of power:

"So also the tongue is a small member, yet it boasts of great exploits. How great a forest is set ablaze by a small fire! And the tongue is a fire . . . With it we bless the Lord and Father, and with it we curse those who are made in the likeness of God. From the same mouth come blessing and cursing. My brothers and sisters, this ought not to be so. " (Jas 3:5–6, 9–10)

Loving God, help my voice to be both pleasant and gentle in the way that I speak to and about others, so that I am always respectful of everyone I meet.

Please bless all those who use their voices in many different ways or who help others to use their voices, including orators and politicians, those who work with microphones and telephones, and teachers and speech pathologists, who help others to be able to speak clearly and correctly. Bless those who are unable to use their voices or who must use artificial devices to speak.

Thank You for the amazing gift of my voice; help me to use it to praise You and to help others understand one another and Your love for them. Amen.

CHAPTER 6

Photograph: In God's Image

MATERIALS AT HAND: A favorite photograph, whether alone or in a frame or an album, and a candle as a prayer focus.

CENTERING (Light the candle and say with your hands spread open:)

Loving God, Creator of all that is,
here I am—today, in this place,
with all the senses you have given me.
Help me to use them to experience You more deeply.
You are present everywhere around me;
open me to know more of the many ways
that your goodness surrounds me.
Thank you for this time to be with you and to listen to you.
Amen.

SAVORING:

For a moment, look at this photograph as a series of shapes and forms on a flat surface, either in shades of black and white or color. Squinting may help with this step. Notice what shapes and lines there are in the photo and where your eye is drawn when you look at the image. Is the focal point a face? A house or other building? A lake or mountain? Or what?

In the Home and at School

What leads your eye to that focal point? Is there a path, a line that your eye follows to get there?

If there were someone standing beside you that had never seen this photograph before and didn't recognize the image in it, how would you describe the photo? Tell the story of how this picture came to be and why this person, place or thing is so important to you. This story is one of many in your life; we don't often stop to think about the bundle of stories that helps make us who we are.

Now in your imagination try to jump into the time and place of the photo. Try to picture the scene before you as you do, smelling all the smells, hearing all the sounds, trying to let yourself experience where and when this photo was taken. Maybe this reunites you with a loved one who has since died or perhaps this allows you to visit a favorite place you miss. Is there anything you would change in the scene now before you if you could, or do you like things just the way they are as you stand there? Is there anything particular that you would do or say?

Photographs can give us such amazing information about our world and help us with the important job of remembering our stories and who we were and are.

LISTENING:

Listen to one or more of these passages as you watch the candle play across the photo:

Then God said, "Let us make humankind in our image, according to our likeness; and let them have dominion over the fish of the sea, and over the birds of the air, and over the cattle, and over all the wild animals of the earth, and over every creeping thing that creeps upon the earth." So God created humankind in his image, in the image of God he created them; male and female he created them. (Gen 1:26–27)

[Jesus] is the image of the invisible God, the firstborn of all creation; for in him all things in heaven and on earth were created, things visible and invisible, whether thrones or dominions or rulers or powers—all things have been created through him and for him. He himself is before all things, and in him all things hold together. (Col 1:15–17)

Photograph: In God's Image

Now the Lord is the Spirit, and where the Spirit of the Lord is, there is freedom. And all of us, with unveiled faces, seeing the glory of the Lord as though reflected in a mirror, are being transformed into the same image from one degree of glory to another; for this comes from the Lord, the Spirit. (2 Cor 3:17–18)

Let us now sing the praises of famous men, our ancestors in their generations. The Lord apportioned to them great glory, his majesty from the beginning. There were those who ruled in their kingdoms, and made a name for themselves by their valor; those who gave counsel because they were intelligent; those who spoke in prophetic oracles; those who led the people by their counsels and by their knowledge of the people's lore; they were wise in their words of instruction; those who composed musical tunes, or put verses in writing; rich men endowed with resources, living peacefully in their homes—all these were honored in their generations, and were the pride of their times. Some of them have left behind a name, so that others declare their praise. But of others there is no memory; they have perished as though they had never existed; they have become as though they had never been born, they and their children after them. But these also were godly men, whose righteous deeds have not been forgotten; their wealth will remain with their descendants, and their inheritance with their children's children. Their descendants stand by the covenants; their children also, for their sake. Their offspring will continue forever, and their glory will never be blotted out. Their bodies are buried in peace, but their name lives on generation after generation. The assembly declares their wisdom, and the congregation proclaims their praise. (Sir 44:1–15)

CONSIDERING:

Images seem to have always been important to the human spirit, based on the earliest cave paintings and other art that we have found. Although the ancient Jewish tradition could appreciate that humans were made in the image of God, it had a prohibition against having any drawn or carved images of God—such as the idols or statues possessed by other peoples—because no image could adequately represent Yahweh; for them, God was far greater than anything in nature, a being outside and beyond it. They knew that the images we have, our pictures, are indeed powerful for our imagination.

In the Home and at School

In our world today, cameras and the technology of photography have given us some images that are indeed very powerful, and they have allowed us to record some of the most important memories of our collective and private lives, so that we can save them for further generations. The word "camera" comes from *camera obscura*, a dark room or chamber with a pinhole opening—and then later a box with a similar hole—used by artists to help them sketch the scenes before them long before film was invented.

In the late 18th century scientists began to experiment with the known sensitivity to light of certain chemicals, and throughout the 19th century the photographic process was gradually perfected, although it was largely the domain of a few professionals because of the expensive and bulky equipment needed. The twentieth century saw the advent of portable cameras for home use, flash bulbs, the wide availability of black and white as well as color film, instant and digital cameras, as well as many other important innovations. Photography took its place as an art form in the twentieth century, and photojournalism has literally changed the way we see our world.

Try to remember the first camera you saw or had, and try to imagine the ways in which the photos and images that you have seen have changed your life. Their impact on us has been so great that it's hard to even begin to get "the whole picture."

RESPONDING:

The process of photography can provide several helpful "images" for examining our lives and our spirituality. Just as a camera can help us look more clearly and more lastingly at what is right before us, the notions of lenses, lighting and film may help us examine our lives.

A photographer may use different lenses, depending on the kind of view desired and the distance to the subject of the photo. Think about your own "lenses" and see whether the "focus" in your life is as clear and sharp right now as you would like it to be. For example, are there areas of your life that are distracting you from what's really important for you? Also, do you need to work on your own flexibility, your willingness to "change lenses" when necessary? Do you, instead, insist that life always be the same, without much change?

Photograph: In God's Image

The lighting in a photograph can make a big difference; it may highlight aspects that weren't visible before, that were "in the dark." Are there parts of your life that need "better lighting," people or situations that you need to be more aware of and not ignore? How can you respond to those parts of your life that have been somewhat neglected, once you are more aware of them?

The "film" for the camera of your life is your memories. Are you grateful for all the memories in your life—even the painful ones—because all of them are what help make you who you are? What memories stand out now as you think about your life and how God has been a part of it all along?

God of all memories and images, thank you for all those who have been a part of my life and have helped me remember my life and who I am. Thank you, too, for photographers and those who make and work with photo equipment and supplies.

Please help me to remember that I am made in Your image and that You are the "focus" of my life and part of all my memories whenever I see a photograph. Amen.

CHAPTER 7

Book: In the Book of Life

Materials at hand: A book or a favorite bookmark, with a candle as a prayer focus.

CENTERING (Light the candle and say with your hands spread open:)

Loving God, Creator of all that is,
here I am—today, in this place,
with all the senses you have given me.
Help me to use them to experience you more deeply.
You are present everywhere around me;
open me to know more of the many ways
that your goodness surrounds me.
Thank you for this time to be with you and to listen to you.
Amen.

SAVORING:

Open the book to a page at random or place the book so that you can't see the title for now, or if you have a bookmark, place it before you. Notice how the candle plays across the book or bookmark, and try to imagine having nothing more than candlelight to read by when it's dark, as many peoples have experienced until the invention of electric lights.

Book: In the Book of Life

As you gently touch the book or bookmark, do it first with your eyes closed to focus on your sense of touch. Notice the feel of the pages and the binding, if you have a book or books before you. What are your fingers noticing that your eyes have not noticed before?

What a wonderful gift lies under your fingers; think of all the kinds of books that have been produced throughout the ages, from those that were painfully hand-copied to those now rapidly published through computer technology. We may not often think about the "technology" of books, but they have changed our lives and the way we look at every aspect of our world, in more ways than we can begin to imagine.

Choose a sentence or two at random from the book if you have one at hand—or perhaps from memory, if not. What an incredible experience it is to be able to see these marks on paper and understand the thought that lies behind them, a thought that is communicated to any reader who knows that language and picks up this pack of assembled paper! In a sense, a private world is created between an author and a reader whenever that reader encounters the written word in a book, even if it is a book read aloud.

What is your favorite book and why? Or what book or books have made an important impact on your life? Again, why is that? Are there any favorite characters that stand out as heroes or heroines for you? What kind of books appeal to you? Which don't appeal? If you were ever to write a book, what would it be about?

Books *are* truly amazing; they give us a look into worlds far beyond our own.

LISTENING:

Listen to one or more of these passages as you watch the candle play across the book or bookmark:

Then I said, "Here I am; in the scroll of the book it is written of me. I delight to do your will, O my God; your law is within my heart." (Ps 40:7-8)

I praise you, for I am fearfully and wonderfully made . . . . My frame was not hidden from you, when I was being made in secret, intricately woven in the depths of the earth. Your eyes beheld my unformed substance. In your book were written all the days that were formed for me, when none of them as yet existed. (Ps 139:14–16)

In the fourth year of King Jehoiakim son of Josiah of Judah, this word came to Jeremiah from the LORD: Take a scroll and write on it all the words that I have spoken to you against Israel and Judah and all the nations, from the day I spoke to you, from the days of Josiah until today. It may be that when the house of Judah hears of all the disasters that I intend to do to them, all of them may turn from their evil ways, so that I may forgive their iniquity and their sin. Then Jeremiah called Baruch son of Neriah, and Baruch wrote on a scroll at Jeremiah's dictation all the words of the LORD that he had spoken to him.... And [then] Baruch son of Neriah did all that the prophet Jeremiah ordered him about reading from the scroll the words of the LORD in the Lord's house . . . .

[The local officials heard the words of the scroll and] went to the court of the king; and they reported all the words to the king.

Then the king sent Jehudi to get the scroll, and he . . . read it to the king and all the officials who stood beside the king. Now the king was sitting in his winter apartment (it was the ninth month), and there was a fire burning in the brazier before him. As Jehudi read three or four columns, the king would cut them off with a penknife and throw them into the fire in the brazier, until the entire scroll was consumed in the fire that was in the brazier. Yet neither the king, nor any of his servants who heard all these words, was alarmed, nor did they tear their garments . . . .

Now, after the king had burned the scroll with the words that Baruch wrote at Jeremiah's dictation, the word of the LORD came to Jeremiah: Take another scroll and write on it all the former words that were in the first scroll, which King Jehoiakim of Judah has burned . . . Then Jeremiah took another scroll and gave it to the secretary Baruch son of Neriah, who wrote on it at Jeremiah's dictation all the words of the scroll that King Jehoiakim of Judah had burned in the fire; and many similar words were added to them. [Jer 36:1–4, 8, 20–24, 27–28, 32]

When he came to Nazareth, where he had been brought up, he went to the synagogue on the sabbath day, as was his custom. He stood up to read, and the scroll of the prophet Isaiah was given to him. He unrolled the scroll and found the place where it was written: "The Spirit of the Lord is upon me, because he has anointed me to bring good news to the poor. He has sent me to proclaim release to the captives and recovery of sight to the blind, to let the oppressed go free, to proclaim the year of the Lord's favor." And he rolled up the scroll, gave it back to the attendant, and sat down. The eyes of all in the synagogue were fixed on him. Then he began to say to them, "Today this scripture has been fulfilled in your hearing." (Luke 4:16–21)

This is the disciple who is testifying to these things and has written them, and we know that his testimony is true. But there are also many other things that Jesus did; if every one of them were written down, I suppose that the world itself could not contain the books that would be written. (John 21:24–25)

CONSIDERING:

Books have a long history in both the East and the West. They began with the clay tablets and styluses used among the peoples of ancient Mesopotamia and, later, scrolls of papyrus rolled around sticks in Egypt, Greece and Rome. Because of papyrus' fragile nature, parchment, made from specially prepared animal skins, had almost entirely replaced it as a material for manuscripts by the fourth century AD.

At about the same time the rectangular codex, a small notebook made of folded larger pages sewn together or held together with wooden rings, became popular in the West and represented a big improvement over the scroll because it allowed the reader to find a place in the text and to refer ahead and back.

Meanwhile, in the Eastern cultures books were usually written on strips of silk or on paper, which had been discovered there in the second century. The Chinese were also printing from wooden blocks by the ninth century and from movable type by the eleventh century. These improvements over handwritten copying as a means of production would only make it to Europe in the fifteenth century, when Johannes Gutenberg published the Bible with movable type, an innovation which would help change Western civilization in many ways.

The printing press considerably reduced the cost of producing books, and it was followed by more changes in the production and the format of books through the Renaissance period. By the time of the Industrial

Revolution this process became more mechanized, and many further refinements have occurred since then, including the current technology which allows publishing on demand.

Today, books still seem to be able to hold their own against other electronic media. It's hard to imagine the world we live in without the libraries of books that have helped make it all possible.

RESPONDING:

Toward the end of the book of Revelation—and of the New Testament—books are a part of the scene about the Final Judgment. The vision is a powerful one: "I saw the dead, great and small, standing before the throne, and books were opened. Also another book was opened, the book of life. And the dead were judged according to their works, as recorded in the books." (Rev 20:12)

How will I—how do I now—look in the "book of life"? If someone were to write a book about my life so far, what would a good title for it be? What am I most proud of having done or been in my life? What am I least proud of or do I regret? If I think about each day as a page in the book of my life, how well would this day help toward "writing" what I'd like to say?

How important is the Bible, the most widely distributed book in the world, to the "book" of my life? What is my favorite passage from scripture? What part or parts are the hardest for me to hear? Is it because this is the most challenging to me? Perhaps I can plan to spend some time with scripture, considering it as a love letter from God—even the difficult parts. Maybe I need to look at joining a bible study or doing some reading on the Bible so that I understand and appreciate it more.

Loving God of volumes and editions, of proofs and paperbacks, please bless all those who write, edit, publish and print books, as well as those who sell, read, and work with books in research or as librarians. Bless, too, those who study and learn from books, both paper and in electronic format. In a special way please be with those who have little or no exposure or access to books, including your word of life in the Bible.

Please help the peoples of the world to continue to use books and the knowledge within them to build bridges of understanding of one another and not to use them to condemn and to wall one another out. Amen.

CHAPTER 8

Map or Globe: Where Can I Go?

MATERIALS AT HAND: A map or globe, with a candle as a prayer focus.

CENTERING (Light the candle and say with your hands spread open:)

Loving God, Creator of all that is,
here I am—today, in this place,
with all the senses you have given me.
Help me to use them to experience you more deeply.
You are present everywhere around me;
open me to know more of the many ways
that your goodness surrounds me.
Thank you for this time to be with you and to listen to you.
Amen.

SAVORING:

As you consider the map or globe before you, try not to focus on the specific information on the map, but rather on it as an example of a map. First, take a look at the folded map or at the globe without spinning it and consider the possibilities before you. With enough time, energy and money you could travel wherever the map before you might take you, with amazing adventures in the process. Depending on your needs and

In the Home and at School

time restrictions, you could either travel wherever your journey happens to take you or on a carefully planned itinerary.

As you open the map or spin the globe, notice how the possibilities of where you can go or how much you are aware of "unfold" before you. Still without paying close attention to the specifics on the map before you, use your finger to "travel" along roads or across borders, "seeing" rivers and lakes and possibly mountains as you do so. How does the "journey" feel? Try to imagine what you might see, hear and even feel along your journey.

Do you enjoy reading maps or dislike doing so? What do you most like about travel and what do you like the least? What was the most favorite trip you have ever taken and why? What about the least favorite trip? Is there somewhere you have always wanted to go and never been to? What is it, and why do you want to go there?

Maps give us a "world" of information about where we are and where we want to go that is easy to take for granted.

LISTENING:

Listen to one or more of these passages as you watch the candle play across the map or globe:

Set up road markers for yourself, make yourself guideposts; consider well the highway, the road by which you went. (Jer 31:21)

Jesus [said], "A man was going down from Jerusalem to Jericho, and fell into the hands of robbers, who stripped him, beat him, and went away, leaving him half dead. Now by chance a priest was going down that road; and when he saw him, he passed by on the other side. So likewise a Levite, when he came to the place and saw him, passed by on the other side. But a Samaritan while traveling came near him; and when he saw him, he was moved with pity. He went to him and bandaged his wounds, having poured oil and wine on them. Then he put him on his own animal, brought him to an inn, and took care of him. The next day he took out two denarii, gave them to the innkeeper, and said, 'Take care of him; and when I come back, I will repay you whatever more you spend.' Which of these three, do you think, was a neighbor to the man who fell into the

Map or Globe: Where Can I Go?

hands of the robbers?" He said, "The one who showed him mercy." Jesus said to him, "Go and do likewise." (Luke 10:30–37)

Enter through the narrow gate; for the gate is wide and the road is easy that leads to destruction, and there are many who take it. For the gate is narrow and the road is hard that leads to life, and there are few who find it. (Matt 7:13–14)

Now on that same day two of them were going to a village called Emmaus, about seven miles from Jerusalem, and talking with each other about all these things that had happened. While they were talking and discussing, Jesus himself came near and went with them, but their eyes were kept from recognizing him. And he said to them, "What are you discussing with each other while you walk along?" They stood still, looking sad. Then one of them, whose name was Cleopas, answered him, "Are you the only stranger in Jerusalem who does not know the things that have taken place there in these days?" He asked them, "What things?" They replied, "The things about Jesus of Nazareth, who was a prophet mighty in deed and word before God and all the people, and how our chief priests and leaders handed him over to be condemned to death and crucified him. But we had hoped that he was the one to redeem Israel. Yes, and besides all this, it is now the third day since these things took place. Moreover, some women of our group astounded us. They were at the tomb early this morning, and when they did not find his body there, they came back and told us that they had indeed seen a vision of angels who said that he was alive. Some of those who were with us went to the tomb and found it just as the women had said; but they did not see him."

. . . As they came near the village to which they were going, he walked ahead as if he were going on. But they urged him strongly, saying, "Stay with us, because it is almost evening and the day is now nearly over." So he went in to stay with them. When he was at the table with them, he took bread, blessed and broke it, and gave it to them. Then their eyes were opened, and they recognized him; and he vanished from their sight. They said to each other, "Were not our hearts burning within us while he was talking to us on the road, while he was opening the scriptures to us?" (Luke 24:13–24, 28–32)

In the Home and at School

Comfort, O comfort my people, says your God.... A voice cries out: "In the wilderness prepare the way of the LORD, make straight in the desert a highway for our God. Every valley shall be lifted up, and every mountain and hill be made low; the uneven ground shall become level, and the rough places a plain. Then the glory of the LORD shall be revealed, and all people shall see it together, for the mouth of the LORD has spoken.".... A highway shall be there, and it shall be called the Holy Way; the unclean shall not travel on it, but it shall be for God's people; no traveler, not even fools, shall go astray. (Isa 40:1,3–5;35:8)

... search, and you will find ... (Matt 7:7)

[Jesus said,]" ... no one can come to me unless it is granted by the Father." Because of this many of his disciples turned back and no longer went about with him. So Jesus asked the twelve, "Do you also wish to go away?" Simon Peter answered him, "Lord, to whom can we go? You have the words of eternal life. (John 6:65–68)

Teach me your way, O LORD, that I may walk in your truth; give me an undivided heart to revere your name. (Ps 86:11)

Thomas said to [Jesus], "Lord, we do not know where you are going. How can we know the way?" Jesus said to him, "I am the way, and the truth, and the life. No one comes to the Father except through me. If you know me, you will know my Father also. From now on you do know him and have seen him." (John 14:5–7)

CONSIDERING:

It is easy for us to take the accuracy of the maps we use for granted, but for much of human history there was far less information to work with, despite many attempts beginning with the earliest civilizations. The Babylonians were making maps as early as 2300 BC on clay tiles, and we have maps from ancient China on silk that go back to the second century BC. Both the Mayan and Inca civilizations were using maps by the twelfth century AD, and the early Greeks also made important early charts and maps.

After the fall of the Roman Empire most map-making ceased in Europe, except for fairly accurate maps of the seas by sailors, first Arabian

Map or Globe: Where Can I Go?

and later European. But by the eighteenth century the major scientific principles of map-making were established. In our times aerial and satellite photography, as well as computers, have helped make maps far more accurate than early cartographers—the technical name for map makers—could have dreamed of.

Maps may be used for many purposes, from natural formations to products and resources to political boundaries, and therefore can highlight different features of the area being charted. Although most parts of the world are now accurately charted, there still remain some areas, such as parts of Antarctica, that need further surveying.

In the New Testament, the reader of the Acts of the Apostles almost needs a map to follow the journeys of Saint Paul, who traveled throughout the Mediterranean area, and perhaps elsewhere, sharing the good news of Christ. We also learn In the book of Acts that the early Christians, before they were called by that name, were merely known as the followers of The Way. In a sense, being on the way and a traveler has always been important to Christians, as we see in the long tradition of a pilgrimage.

RESPONDING:

The image of a journey and a map gives us a helpful way to think about the pilgrimage of our lives and how and where it is going. It may even be helpful to draw a time line of your life and what the ups and downs of it have been so far.

However, the book of Sirach reminds us that what we may think of as a problem or a tragedy may actually turn out to be a blessing, depending on whether we learn from that "obstacle": "Do not go on a path full of hazards, and do not stumble at an obstacle twice. Do not be overconfident on a smooth road, and give good heed to your paths." (Sir 32:20–22)

It would be nice to have a "map" of our lives and of God's will for each of us, to know exactly what will happen and be able to prepare for it, but that's not the way God operates in our lives. Travel—and life—always seems to involve the unexpected, no matter how much information we think we have. How are you at "asking for directions"—getting help or advice when needed?

Loving God of our comings and goings, of all places and peoples, bless all those who make maps and those who use them to help study other parts of the world. Bless all travelers and those who provide hospitality to travelers. Please keep all those who are traveling this day safe and able to return home safely. Please bless those in all parts of our world that don't have the basics for a healthy existence and help the rest of us to become more aware of the single planet that we all share as home.

Please help me to remember that coming home to you and your love is my ultimate "destination" whenever I see a map. Amen.

I will tell you what wisdom is and how she came to be, and I will hide no secrets from you, but I will trace her course from the beginning of creation, and make knowledge of her clear, and I will not pass by the truth; nor will I travel in the company of sickly envy, for envy does not associate with wisdom. (Wisdom 6:22–23)

CHAPTER 9

Letters of the Alphabet: I Am the Alpha and the Omega

MATERIALS AT HAND: A paper on which you have written some or all of the letters of the alphabet, perhaps in various styles with pen, pencil, crayon, or marker, and a candle as a prayer focus.

CENTERING (Light the candle and say with your hands spread open:)

Loving God, Creator of all that is,
here I am—today, in this place,
with all the senses you have given me.
Help me to use them to experience you more deeply.
You are present everywhere around me;
open me to know more of the many ways
that your goodness surrounds me.
Thank you for this time to be with you and to listen to you.
Amen.

SAVORING:

Look at the letters written out before you. If you had never been educated or had been educated with a completely different alphabet or on a different planet (if that were possible), you would see on this page a set of random markings with interesting shapes. As it is, you see before you the building blocks, not only for important communication between people but for all of literature, as we know it.

Take your finger and trace around each letter, saying to yourself as you do, its sound or a word that begins with it. Do you have a favorite letter? If so, which one is it? Is it one of your initials or why is it your favorite? Do you have any memories of learning the alphabet and the song to help you know your letters? If you had the opportunity to put the letters of the alphabet in a different order than the way they are now, how would you arrange them?

Do you have a favorite word? If so, what is it? If not, is there a word or two which fascinates you? Try to make up a nonsense word with the letters before you and give it a silly meaning.

In a sense, what you see before you are pieces of a puzzle that can be arranged in so many ways, to form everything from love notes to terrorist ransom demands. These marks on paper can be very powerful tools.

LISTENING:

Listen to one or more of these passages as you watch the candle play across the paper with the letters of the alphabet:

In the beginning was the Word, and the Word was with God, and the Word was God. He was in the beginning with God. All things came into being through him, and without him not one thing came into being. What has come into being in him was life, and the life was the light of all people . . . And the Word became flesh and lived among us, and we have seen his glory, the glory as of a father's only son, full of grace and truth. (John 1:1–4, 14)

Now the whole earth had one language and the same words. And as they migrated from the east, they came upon a plain in the land of Shinar and settled there . . . Then they said, "Come, let us build ourselves a city, and a tower with its top in the heavens, and let us make a name for ourselves; otherwise we shall be scattered abroad upon the face of the whole earth." The LORD came down to see the city and the tower, which mortals had built. And the LORD said, "Look, they are one people, and they have all one language; and this is only the beginning of what they will do; nothing that they propose to do will now be impossible for them. Come, let us go down, and confuse their language there, so that they will not understand

Letters of the Alphabet: I Am the Alpha and the Omega

one another's speech." So the LORD scattered them abroad from there over the face of all the earth, and they left off building the city. Therefore it was called Babel, because there the LORD confused the language of all the earth; and from there the LORD scattered them abroad over the face of all the earth. (Gen 11:1–2, 4–9)

When the day of Pentecost had come, they were all together in one place ... All of them were filled with the Holy Spirit and began to speak in other languages, as the Spirit gave them ability. Now there were devout Jews from every nation under heaven living in Jerusalem. And at this sound the crowd gathered and was bewildered, because each one heard them speaking in the native language of each. Amazed and astonished, they asked, "Are not all these who are speaking Galileans? And how is it that we hear, each of us, in our own native language?" All were amazed and perplexed, saying to one another, "What does this mean?" (Acts 2:1, 4–8, 12)

Hear, O Israel: The LORD is our God, the LORD alone. You shall love the LORD your God with all your heart, and with all your soul, and with all your might. Keep these words that I am commanding you today in your heart. (Deut 6:4–6)

If you abide in me, and my words abide in you, ask for whatever you wish, and it will be done for you. (John 15:7)

Likewise the Spirit helps us in our weakness; for we do not know how to pray as we ought, but that very Spirit intercedes with sighs too deep for words. (Rom 8:26)

CONSIDERING:

The word "alphabet" comes from the first two letters of the Greek one: Alpha and Beta. (The last letter of that same alphabet is the letter Omega.)

In an alphabet that is phonetic, like ours, each letter should indicate a sound which in turn forms a word, a goal which is most closely achieved by the Korean alphabet. In most phonetic alphabets one letter can stand for several sounds, as is true in the English alphabet.

Other systems of writing are pictographic or ideographic, where a symbol or picture stands for the word for that object, such as a simple picture of a house or a sun to stand for that concept, as we might see in a language like Chinese. Some alphabets only had—and some still only have—consonants; Hebrew and Arabic languages, for example, only have vowels as points or dashes.

Our present alphabets have evolved gradually, descending from a few root languages. Some languages are written left to right, while others read right to left. Each individual letter has a fascinating history as it has evolved, usually from a pictographic symbol to a phonetic one today. Some alphabets have been created artificially for people who were otherwise illiterate or previously using foreign alphabets. The written forms of a language and its alphabet undergo modifications and changes as the language changes with the people and the times, although the spoken language changes far more quickly. Unfortunately, as cultures change and intersect with one another, many languages and their concepts—and at times their alphabets—are disappearing.

RESPONDING:

Our alphabets give us tools to write and think about all kinds of things, "from A to Z," as we say. Take some time to write to someone you care about or to write in your journal, appreciating anew the amazing tools that we have in an alphabet that allows us to put thoughts into marks on paper.

We are reminded in several places in the last book of our Bible, the book of Revelation, that God is a part of all of life: "I am the Alpha and the Omega, the first and the last, the beginning and the end." (22:13) and "'I am the Alpha and the Omega' says the Lord God, who is and who was and who is to come, the Almighty." (1:8)

Loving God of all that is written and spoken, help us to remember that you are the beginning, the middle and the end of all that we do and are. Please bless all those who use various alphabets: all writers and poets, all students—especially those studying another language or alphabet, all the teachers who help with literacy and teach languages, all those who do typesetting and work on dictionaries and other language resources, all those who work with alphabetizing materials, from librarians and researchers of all kinds to any clerks.

And please bless in a special way those whose culture and language and alphabet are disappearing as our world changes. Help us all to use our alphabets and our languages to speak peace and love to one another, rather than to condemn and to destroy. Amen.

CHAPTER 10

Flag or Symbol: More Than Meets the Eye

Materials at hand: A candle as a prayer focus, a small flag if you have one or something with a team insignia or a company's design on it.

CENTERING (Light the candle and say with your hands spread open:)

Loving God, Creator of all that is,
here I am—today, in this place,
with all the senses you have given me.
Help me to use them to experience you more deeply
you are present everywhere around me;
open me to know more of the many ways
that your goodness surrounds me.
Thank you for this time to be with you and to listen to you.
Amen.

SAVORING:

Whatever the flag or insignia is, lay it before you and let your eyes take in the design and texture of it, predicting what your other senses, especially your sense of touch will experience. Then close your eyes and see if the information was what you expected it to be. What do your fingers tell you? Are there many differences in texture within this symbolic object? What about your ears? Does the symbol make any noise when handled?

In the Home and at School

Any information from your nose about this symbol? We tend to focus on the visual importance of a symbol, but maybe there's other information this one can give you when you're not looking at it.

Consider what this symbol means to you and the history that has made it important to you. Recall all the times that this insignia has been important in the past to you. Then set aside for now whatever the symbol means for you and consider instead how it might appear to someone who has no idea of its symbolic connections. For example, would that person see a bit of cloth with red and white stripes and stars in the corner on a blue background or a strange insignia or what? Apart from their stories and their meaning for us, our symbols may not seem like much, but because of the shared history they represent, they have great significance to us.

LISTENING:

Listen to one or more of these passages as you watch the candle play across the flag or other symbol:

Then God said to Noah and to his sons with him, ... "This is the sign of the covenant that I make between me and you and every living creature that is with you, for all future generations: I have set my bow in the clouds, and it shall be a sign of the covenant between me and the earth. When I bring clouds over the earth and the bow is seen in the clouds, I will remember my covenant that is between me and you and every living creature of all flesh; and the waters shall never again become a flood to destroy all flesh. (Genesis 9:8, 12–15)

The LORD said to Moses: you yourself are to speak to the Israelites: "You shall keep my sabbaths, for this is a sign between me and you throughout your generations, given in order that you may know that I, the LORD, sanctify you. You shall keep the sabbath, because it is holy for you; everyone who profanes it shall be put to death; whoever does any work on it shall be cut off from among the people. Six days shall work be done, but the seventh day is a sabbath of solemn rest, holy to the LORD; whoever does any work on the sabbath day shall be put to death. Therefore the Israelites shall keep the sabbath, observing the sabbath throughout their generations, as a perpetual covenant. It is a sign forever between me and

Flag or Symbol: More Than Meets the Eye

the people of Israel that in six days the LORD made heaven and earth, and on the seventh day he rested, and was refreshed." (Exodus 31:12–17)

O God, the insolent rise up against me; a band of ruffians seeks my life, and they do not set you before them. But you, O Lord, are a God merciful and gracious, slow to anger and abounding in steadfast love and faithfulness. Turn to me and be gracious to me; give your strength to your servant; save the child of your serving girl. Show me a sign of your favor, so that those who hate me may see it and be put to shame, because you, LORD, have helped me and comforted me. (Ps 86:14–17)

While [Jesus] was still speaking, Judas, one of the twelve, arrived; with him was a large crowd with swords and clubs, from the chief priests and the elders of the people. Now the betrayer had given them a sign, saying, "The one I will kiss is the man; arrest him." At once he came up to Jesus and said, "Greetings, Rabbi!" and kissed him. Jesus said to him, "Friend, do what you are here to do." Then they came and laid hands on Jesus and arrested him. (Matthew 26:47–50)

[Jesus] cried with a loud voice, "Lazarus, come out!" The dead man came out, his hands and feet bound with strips of cloth, and his face wrapped in a cloth. Jesus said to them, "Unbind him, and let him go." Many of the Jews therefore, who had come with Mary and had seen what Jesus did, believed in him. But some of them went to the Pharisees and told them what he had done. So the chief priests and the Pharisees called a meeting of the council, and said, "What are we to do? This man is performing many signs.

If we let him go on like this, everyone will believe in him, and the Romans will come and destroy both our holy place and our nation." (John 11:43–48)

Now Jesus did many other signs in the presence of his disciples, which are not written in this book. But these are written so that you may come to believe that Jesus is the Messiah, the Son of God, and that through believing you may have life in his name. (John 20:30–31)

In the Home and at School

CONSIDERING:

Symbols of one kind or another actually surround us every day, from language and writing we use to signs and logos for many different products and companies. Our use of symbols is so important to who we are as humans that there is a term for those who, as a result of a brain disorder, perhaps from an injury, have lost their memory of the meaning of symbols: sensory aphasia. The victim can hear sounds, for example, but cannot understand a single spoken word.

We often use symbols in our personal and national lives. Whether it's a card, a rose or other flower or a favorite object as a gift, we often try to say the unsayable to those we love. National symbols, such as the various flags of the world or images such as the hammer and sickle or the swastika, often have long and complex histories. We are quite aware of symbols in the fields of mathematics and science, but most fields have their special symbols, including religious traditions. For the most part these uses are not controversial; however, there was even a movement to condemn the use of religious images and statues– by a group called the Iconoclasts—that was especially strong in the eighth and ninth centuries in the Byzantine Empire

In the Catholic tradition, seven symbols and actions– seven sacraments– have emerged as the way to express the life of faith. Several of these are shared by many other Christian denominations, especially Baptism. In the Hebrew scriptures there are many signs and symbols, from the burning bush that Moses sees in Exodus chapter three to the sign of circumcision to the plagues that are sent to convince Pharaoh to let the Israelites go. In the New Testament Jesus performs many signs and cures, especially in John's gospel, that tell of God's healing power, and one of Jesus' warnings is to beware of those who perform false signs that may lead people astray.

RESPONDING:

God of all signs and symbols, help me to see more of the ways that the signs of your life and love are all around me. Bless those who make and sell symbols of all kinds, from greeting cards to jewelry to letter jackets to uniforms and even those in advertising. And be with especially those who serve in the name of their flag and proudly wear that symbol or the symbol of the police or fire department of their area. Bless those innocents and their families that have been killed in the name of various flags and the countries they represent. And also bless those who play for a team or who root for them and who proudly wear the symbol of that team.

Help me to appreciate more the symbols in my life when I see this symbol and to use those symbols well to share your love and peace with others. Amen.

CHAPTER 11

Eraser: Wipe Away My Offenses

Materials at hand: An eraser, either a rubber one—separate or attached to a pencil—or a chalkboard one, and a candle as a prayer focus.

CENTERING (Light the candle and say with your hands spread open:)

Loving God, Creator of all that is,
here I am—today, in this place,
with all the senses you have given me.
Help me to use them to experience you more deeply
you are present everywhere around me;
open me to know more of the many ways
that your goodness surrounds me.
Thank you for this time to be with you and to listen to you.
Amen.

SAVORING:

Take a look at the eraser before you, whether rubber for erasing pencil marks or a felt one for erasing chalk or a dry marker. Before touching it, try to predict what your fingers will experience.

As you touch the eraser, close your eyes so that you can be more aware of the information from your fingers. Notice the texture of the eraser; each kind has to have a certain amount of "give" in order to be

Eraser: Wipe Away My Offenses

able to do its job: rubbing off marks. Can you remember using an eraser with a pencil in school, knowing that when you made a mistake, whether in writing, spelling or arithmetic, it was there? You knew that if you made a mistake, you could make it right again, and the error would disappear as though it had never existed. Do you remember what kind of eraser you had and where you kept it?

Now imagine a piece of paper or a chalkboard on which has been written some of the mistakes that you have made in your life, some of the poor choices perhaps you wish you could go back and change. Recall for a moment what might be on such a list for you. Imagine also that you are God for a moment, taking the eraser before you and wiping away those mistakes, worries, even sins, so that they are gone, as though they had never existed. Notice how it feels to know that those mistakes are "off the record." Is there a feeling of relief at not having to think about them or spend any energy regretting them any more?

It's certainly good to have erasers—in life, as well as in school!

LISTENING:

Listen to one or more of these passages as you watch the candle play across the eraser:

Then the Lord GOD will wipe away the tears from all faces, and the disgrace of his people he will take away from all the earth, for the LORD has spoken. It will be said on that day, Lo, this is our God; we have waited for him, so that he might save us. This is the LORD for whom we have waited; let us be glad and rejoice in his salvation. (Is 25:8–9)

If we say that we have no sin, we deceive ourselves, and the truth is not in us. If we confess our sins, he who is faithful and just will forgive us our sins and cleanse us from all unrighteousness. (1 John 1:8–9)

Then some people came, bringing to him a paralyzed man, carried by four of them. And when they could not bring him to Jesus because of the crowd, they removed the roof above him; and after having dug through it, they let down the mat on which the paralytic lay. When Jesus saw their faith, he said to the paralytic, "Son, your sins are forgiven." Now some of the scribes were sitting there, questioning in their hearts, "Why does this fellow speak in this way? It is blasphemy! Who can forgive sins but God alone?" At once Jesus perceived in his spirit that they were discussing these questions among themselves; and he said to them, "Why do you raise such questions in your hearts? Which is easier, to say to the paralytic, 'Your sins are forgiven,' or to say, 'Stand up and take your mat and walk'? But so that you may know that the Son of Man has authority on earth to forgive sins"—he said to the paralytic—"I say to you, stand up, take your mat and go to your home." (Mark 2:3–11)

When they came to the place that is called The Skull, they crucified Jesus there with the criminals, one on his right and one on his left. Then Jesus said, "Father, forgive them; for they do not know what they are doing." (Luke 23:33–34)

CONSIDERING:

In a sense, erasers are the reason for our name for rubber. The early European explorers to Central and South America found the natives there playing with and using a substance that they called *cahuchu*, which means weeping wood. But in 1770 the English chemist Joseph Priestly discovered that the material could be used to rub out pencil marks, and so the English word for this substance became "rubber."

That substance wasn't known in ancient Israel, but the reality of "rubbing out" or forgiving sins was. God was the one who could forgive sins and mistakes and no longer hold it against the people, and when Jesus claimed to forgive sins, his Jewish audience heard that as his claiming to be God, which was hard for them to accept, and that eventually resulted in Jesus' being crucified—after he forgave those directly responsible for his death from the cross.

Forgiveness and reconciliation is something we often do very poorly—whether it's forgiving those who hurt us personally or our political or social enemies or even ourselves. Some ethnic groups may have longer memories than others; the definition of Irish Alzheimer's, for example, is forgetting everything but the grudges!

There *is* a certain amount of friction and rubbing necessary in order to erase something; maybe part of the problem with reconciliation for us is that we resist the "friction" of change, and that keeps us from forgiving ourselves and others more readily.

Eraser: Wipe Away My Offenses

RESPONDING:

The implications for our lives of God's forgiving love are fairly clear, although we don't usually want to hear them. First of all, we need to forgive ourselves, since God has forgiven us, which can at times be the hardest of all. But that's just the beginning.

The book of Sirach puts it this way: "Forgive your neighbor the wrong he has done, and then your sins will be pardoned when you pray. Does anyone harbor anger against another, and expect healing from the Lord? If one has no mercy toward another like himself, can he then seek pardon for his own sins?" (Sir 28:2-4) Paul's letter to the Christians at Colossus puts it quite succinctly: " . . . just as the Lord has forgiven you, so you also must forgive." (Col. 3:13) And the gospel of Matthew gives us a choice: " . . . if you forgive others their trespasses, your heavenly Father will also forgive you; but if you do not forgive others, neither will your Father forgive your trespasses." (Matt 6:14-15)

We hear it again and again in scripture: the implications of God's merciful, forgiving, "erasing" love are that we are to work at the same kind of love for each other, a love that may not approve of some of our dumb choices but keeps on loving us, no matter what we choose.

Peter, perhaps like some of us, wanted to know the outer limits of that forgiving love that we are called to. "Then Peter came and said to him, "Lord, if another member of the church sins against me, how often should I forgive? As many as seven times?" Jesus said to him, "Not seven times, but, I tell you, seventy-seven times." (Matt 18:21-22) And then Jesus went on to tell about the king who decided to settle his accounts but forgave a servant who owed him a large sum after the servant pleaded for mercy. However, this same servant then demanded full payment for a lesser debt from a fellow servant and did not show the same mercy that he had been shown. Jesus ends the story this way: "Then his lord summoned him and said to him, 'You wicked slave! I forgave you all that debt because you pleaded with me. Should you not have had mercy on your fellow slave, as I had mercy on you?' And in anger his lord handed him over to be tortured until he would pay his entire debt. So my heavenly Father will also do to every one of you, if you do not forgive your brother or sister from your heart." (Matt 18:32-35) In other words, Jesus is reminding us that God's forgiveness is endless towards us, and that is our goal with others, too.

In the Home and at School

Loving God of all our choices and errors, of erasers and forgiveness, thank you for all my mistakes; help me to learn from each one and learn to love you and to love *like* you each time I fall short of what I want to do. Please bless all those whom I need to forgive and those who need to forgive me. Bless, too, all those who make and use erasers of all kinds, especially teachers and students. Help me to remember your forgiving love whenever I see an eraser. Amen

Around the House

CHAPTER 12

Ruler: A Generous Measure

Materials at hand: A ruler or tape measure or measuring cups or spoons, and a candle as a prayer focus.

CENTERING (Light the candle and say with your hands spread open:)

Loving God, Creator of all that is,
here I am—today, in this place,
with all the senses you have given me.
Help me to use them to experience you more deeply.
You are present everywhere around me;
open me to know more of the many ways
that your goodness surrounds me.
Thank you for this time to be with you and to listen to you.
Amen.

SAVORING:

Take a look at the instrument of measure before you, whether a ruler or a tape measure, measuring spoons or cups. Think about all the ways we use such tools every day, whether in building, sewing, designing, cooking, getting something to fit where it needs to or even describing something precisely.

Slowly travel the length (or depth) of the measure with your eye, thinking as you do of objects that may be those lengths or those amounts.

Then do the same with your fingers while your eyes are closed, noticing whether there are grooves in the ruler that give your fingers some clue as to how far they've "gone" or markings on the cups or spoons that tell you the amount they can hold.

We use so many of these measuring tools every day without a second thought. Reflect on how important accuracy is in the ways we use these instruments and what kinds of complications can happen when we don't "measure up." These devices are indeed helpful when it "counts."

LISTENING:

Listen to one or more of these passages as you watch the candle play across the measuring tape or ruler, cups or spoons:

Who can measure [God's] majestic power? And who can fully recount his mercies? It is not possible to diminish or increase them, nor is it possible to fathom the wonders of the Lord. When human beings have finished, they are just beginning, and when they stop, they are still perplexed. (Sir 18:5–7)

How weighty to me are your thoughts, O God! How vast is the sum of them! I try to count them—they are more than the sand; I come to the end—I am still with you. (Ps 139:17–18)

I pray that you may have the power to comprehend, with all the saints, what is the breadth and length and height and depth, and to know the love of Christ that surpasses knowledge, so that you may be filled with all the fullness of God. (Eph 3:18–19)

CONSIDERING:

Measuring isn't as easy as it looks; it took a long time to develop basic standardization in the way we measure, whether in length or weight or volume. The early standards of length were the palm or breadth of the hand, the foot, or the cubit, which was the length from the elbow to the tip of the middle finger. The only problem is that we know these distances can vary considerably from one person to another.

In the 1790's the metric system was introduced and adopted by law in France and gradually became the international standard for measurement. Although the United States and Great Britain have held onto measuring in inches, feet, yards, miles, pounds and gallons in the face of several attempts to convert to a fully metric system, these amounts are now officially based on the metric equivalents in order to have an international standard.

We live in a culture that likes to know amounts and numbers—how many were there, what did it cost, what was your score or your grade, how big is it and how far away. But so many parts of our lives *can't* be counted or measured—areas such as friendship, love and faith.

RESPONDING:

When it comes to measuring and weighing, both scripture and our faith call us both to honesty and to not judging others—or ourselves.

Honesty in weighing and measuring was very important in the Old Testament and linked to God's "fairness" to the Jewish people. "You shall not cheat in measuring length, weight, or quantity. you shall have honest balances, honest weights, an honest ephah, and an honest hin: I am the LORD your God, who brought you out of the land of Egypt." (Lev 19:35-36)

In the book of Deuteronomy we also see this theme of the need for fairness in light of the fact that evidently merchants, who had their own set of weights and measures, might at times use a second, unfair set:

"You shall not have in your bag two kinds of weights, large and small. You shall not have in your house two kinds of measures, large and small. You shall have only a full and honest weight; you shall have only a full and honest measure, so that your days may be long in the land that the LORD your God is giving you. For all who do such things, all who act dishonestly, are abhorrent to the LORD your God." (Deut 25:13-16)

Are there any ways that I can work on being more honest and acting with more integrity in my life, not having one set of standards for others and another set for myself?

"Measuring" happens in more ways than just counting inches and pounds. We live in a society that is very competitive and, therefore, quite judgmental. If we're not judging others, their looks or their actions, then we're usually doing the same to ourselves, with even more severity. But Jesus reminds us in Luke's gospel not to judge at all, to remember God's

Around the House

wonderful and gracious generosity and then to act similarly toward others.

"Do not judge, and you will not be judged; do not condemn, and you will not be condemned. Forgive, and you will be forgiven; give, and it will be given to you. A good measure, pressed down, shaken together, running over, will be put into your lap; for the measure you give will be the measure you get back." (Luke 6:37–38)

Generous and gracious God, help me to learn to "measure" with your scale, to not spend my energies judging myself or others. Bless those who work with measures of all kinds every day; keep them fair and honest, especially with the poor. Help me to keep learning about and wondering at your "countless" gifts to me. Amen.

CHAPTER 13

Cup or Mug: Let It Pass from Me

MATERIALS AT HAND: A candle as a prayer focus and a favorite cup or mug.

CENTERING (Light the candle and say with your hands spread open:)

Loving God, Creator of all that is,
here I am—today, in this place,
with all the senses you have given me.
Help me to use them to experience you more deeply.
You are present everywhere around me;
open me to know more of the many ways
that your goodness surrounds me.
Thank you for this time to be with you and to listen to you.
Amen.

SAVORING:

Pretend for a moment that you have never seen this cup before. What do you notice about it at first before ever touching it? Is there a particular design on the outside? Is it especially large or small or unusual in its shape? Just in your imagination for now, reach out to hold the cup; what do think your fingers will experience?

Consider all the times that you have used this mug, perhaps day after day. It has given you faithful service by containing whatever you put inside and waiting until you wanted to drink it. With this in mind, as you close your eyes touch this cup as if you were touching a very holy vessel, eager to take in information through your fingers that your eyes may have missed. Is there a variety to the textures of this cup or is it all the same kind of surface? Are there any chips or cracks in it from all the use you have given it?

Notice more carefully than you may have before how the handle is attached to the cup, and reflect on how its function would be changed if something happened to the handle. Notice how your fingers fit easily into the handle, ready to almost make the cup an extension of your hand.

This cup has been a part of your life, patiently allowing you to nourish yourself with its contents.

LISTENING:

Listen to one or more of these passages as you watch the candle play across the cup:

The LORD is my chosen portion and my cup; you hold my lot . . . I keep the LORD always before me; because he is at my right hand, I shall not be moved. Therefore my heart is glad, and my soul rejoices; my body also rests secure. (Ps 16:5, 8–9)

[Jesus said,] "Woe to you, scribes and Pharisees, hypocrites! For you clean the outside of the cup and of the plate, but inside they are full of greed and self-indulgence. You blind Pharisee! First clean the inside of the cup, so that the outside also may become clean. Woe to you, scribes and Pharisees, hypocrites! For you are like whitewashed tombs, which on the outside look beautiful, but inside they are full of the bones of the dead and of all kinds of filth. So you also on the outside look righteous to others, but inside you are full of hypocrisy and lawlessness." (Matt 23:25–28)

Then the mother of the sons of Zebedee came to [Jesus] with her sons, and kneeling before him, she asked a favor of him. And he said to her, "What do you want?" She said to him, "Declare that these two sons of mine will sit, one at your right hand and one at your left, in your kingdom."

Cup or Mug: Let It Pass from Me

But Jesus answered, "you do not know what you are asking. Are you able to drink the cup that I am about to drink?" They said to him, "We are able."

He said to them, "You will indeed drink my cup, but to sit at my right hand and at my left, this is not mine to grant, but it is for those for whom it has been prepared by my Father." (Matt 20:20–23)

Then [Jesus] took a cup, and after giving thanks he gave it to them, saying, "Drink from it, all of you; for this is my blood of the covenant, which is poured out for many for the forgiveness of sins. I tell you, I will never again drink of this fruit of the vine until that day when I drink it new with you in my Father's kingdom." (Matt 26:27–29)

Then Jesus went with them to a place called Gethsemane; and he said to his disciples, "Sit here while I go over there and pray." He took with him Peter and the two sons of Zebedee, and began to be grieved and agitated.

Then he said to them, "I am deeply grieved, even to death; remain here, and stay awake with me." And going a little farther, he threw himself on the ground and prayed, "My Father, if it is possible, let this cup pass from me; yet not what I want but what you want." (Matt 26:36–39)

What shall I return to the LORD for all his bounty to me? I will lift up the cup of salvation and call on the name of the LORD, I will pay my vows to the LORD in the presence of all his people. (Ps 116:12–14)

CONSIDERING:

Cups of one sort or another have been around since human civilization began, often made from pottery or ceramics—whether earthenware, porcelain or china. These materials consist of certain kinds of clay, fired at high temperatures in kilns and often sealed with a kind of glaze. Cups have also been made from wood and various metals, such pewter, silver or gold, as well as glass—and more recently from plastic or similar resins.

In one way or another, cups echo human hands cupped together to catch water or other liquids. We may also use them at times to store small objects, such as pens and pencils.

Around the House

Today cups may be specially designed to be on the go with us and even to keep our liquids hot or cold on the way. Whether at home or after leaving the house, many people wouldn't know what to do without a cup of coffee or tea first thing in the morning as they start their day.

RESPONDING:

God of all creation, thank you for all the kinds of cups we experience in our lives, for all those who design, make, sell and use cups, for those who serve others by filling or washing their cups, as well as those who are homeless and/or poor and end up begging with a cup. Bless those who work with clay and pottery and those who help to provide cups for those who have none and to give them something to fill their cups. Jesus told us, "For truly I tell you, whoever gives you a cup of water to drink because you bear the name of Christ will by no means lose the reward." (Mark 9:41)

Loving God, thank you for all the ways that you have filled the cup of my life. Please bless those whose "cups" have been especially chipped or cracked; give them the help they need to heal from those hurts and to be able to go on with their lives. And help them—and me—to continue to grow in trust of you. Amen.

Even though I walk through the darkest valley, I fear no evil; for you are with me; your rod and your staff—they comfort me. you prepare a table before me in the presence of my enemies; you anoint my head with oil; my cup overflows. Surely goodness and mercy shall follow me all the days of my life, and I shall dwell in the house of the LORD my whole life long. (Ps 23:4–6)

CHAPTER 14

Door: I Stand and Knock

MATERIALS AT HAND: SIT near a door that you can examine closely, with a candle as a prayer focus.

CENTERING (Light the candle and say with your hands spread open:)

Loving God, Creator of all that is,
here I am—today, in this place,
with all the senses you have given me.
Help me to use them to experience you more deeply.
You are present everywhere around me;
open me to know more of the many ways
that your goodness surrounds me.
Thank you for this time to be with you and to listen to you.
Amen.

SAVORING:

Take a look at the door before you as though you are seeing it for the very first time. Picture the doorway without the door in it and how different that space would seem. Are there any distinctive features to this door that might set it apart from others, even other doors in the same room? Is it painted or does it have a natural finish? Is there any texture to the door or details other than the knob?

Around the House

Before touching the door, predict what your fingers will find and see how well your hands remember what they probably touch quite often. The knob is the part of the door you touch most often; what kind of knob is it? Think of all the hands that have grasped that knob countless times, and think of how hard it would be to open the door without it.

Examine the hinges; do they match the knob? Think of the work these hinges do over and over again without our giving them a second thought. The two parts of each hinge fit together with just the right balance between closeness and distance to allow the door to be solid and yet swing freely.

Notice the rest of the door frame, the strike plate where the latch meets the frame and the trim around the doorway, both just the right size and waiting to receive the door when it closes. As you explore the door with your fingers as well as with your eyes, see if there are any places that you hadn't noticed before, from the latch on the edge of the door to the bottom or top edge of the door.

Now very slowly close and/or open the door, imagining as you do so that you are the door and try to imagine the changes you would be experiencing as you open and close. When the door is closed, there is a separation of space—outside and inside—which no longer exists in the same way when it is open.

Doors seem like simple inventions mechanically, but without them our lives might be quite different.

LISTENING:

Listen to one or more of these passages as you watch the candle play across the door:

When it was evening on that day, the first day of the week, and the doors of the house where the disciples had met were locked for fear of the Jews, Jesus came and stood among them and said, "Peace be with you." After he said this, he showed them his hands and his side. Then the disciples rejoiced when they saw the Lord. (John 20:19–20)

Hear, O Israel: The LORD is our God, the LORD alone. You shall love the LORD your God with all your heart, and with all your soul, and with all your might. Keep these words that I am commanding you today in your heart. Recite them to your children and talk about them when you are at home and when you are away, when you lie down and when you rise. Bind them as a sign on your hand, fix them as an emblem on your forehead, and write them on the doorposts of your house and on your gates. (Deut 6:4–9)

And whenever you pray, do not be like the hypocrites; for they love to stand and pray in the synagogues and at the street corners, so that they may be seen by others. Truly I tell you, they have received their reward. But whenever you pray, go into your room and shut the door and pray to your Father who is in secret; and your Father who sees in secret will reward you. (Matt 6:5–6)

And he said to them, "Suppose one of you has a friend, and you go to him at midnight and say to him, 'Friend, lend me three loaves of bread; for a friend of mine has arrived, and I have nothing to set before him.' And he answers from within, 'Do not bother me; the door has already been locked, and my children are with me in bed; I cannot get up and give you anything.' I tell you, even though he will not get up and give him anything because he is his friend, at least because of his persistence he will get up and give him whatever he needs. "So I say to you, Ask, and it will be given you; search, and you will find; knock, and the door will be opened for you. For everyone who asks receives, and everyone who searches finds, and for everyone who knocks, the door will be opened. (Luke 11:5–10)

CONSIDERING:

The first thing that guests encounter when they come to our house or apartment is a door, and it's the same whenever we go to visit someone else. Doors—and at times the gates to our gardens or yards—are powerful symbols as well as important devices. They separate the outside from the inside, and although we rarely think of it, crossing over the threshold into a home is an important action for both guests and family members. Not only is this threshold the place we welcome guests into our homes and our lives, it is the place where we leave each other and return again at the end of our day or the end of our travels. Some families give each other a blessing, asking God to protect them before leaving the house at the start of the day, since we're never completely sure that we'll all make it back safely at the end of the day.

There are many doors in our homes; how many are there in your house, and which is the most important one to you? Why?

We don't know much about how doors were constructed throughout human history. It seems quite likely that for much of human history doors were a luxury, something that the poor may not have had. Doors can vary widely from flaps on tents to simple curtains of fabric or beads to massive wooden ones with elaborate carvings and precious metals. But whatever their shape, their purpose is the same.

Doors are a symbol of privacy; they can be a means to feel safe from the outside world and from others, but the danger is that they can also be a way to shut others out of our lives.

RESPONDING:

Doors can be important reminders to us of what comes into and goes out of each of us as well as our homes. For example, two different passages in scripture use the image of a door to remind us to watch what we say. Psalm 141 prays, "Set a guard over my mouth, O LORD; keep watch over the door of my lips." (Ps 141:3) And the book of Sirach reminds us, "As you fence in your property with thorns, so make a door and a bolt for your mouth. As you lock up your silver and gold, so make balances and scales for your words." (Sir 28:24–25) Dear God, please help me to watch my comments so that they are always kind and fair.

In the Book of Revelation we find a striking image of God knocking on our door: "Listen! I am standing at the door, knocking; if you hear my voice and open the door, I will come in to you and eat with you, and you with me." (Rev 3:20) This passage reminds us that *we* are the ones who decide how "open" to God our lives will be. Do you want to "open the door" a bit further to God? How, specifically? Is there anyone else in your life that you keep waiting outside your "door?" Why? Would this be a good time to "invite him or her in?"

Loving God of all our comings and goings, thank you for the gift of doors. Bless all those who make doors and locks and hinges and all those who build and design houses and buildings and their doors. Bless abundantly all those who offer hospitality to others, whose door is always open to those in need. And please bless all those who are homeless or refugees, who are without a home or a door of their own. Help them find a place of welcome and a door open to their safety and hope.

Please help me be more aware of the gift of doors and of what I'm keeping in and shutting out of my life, and help me be more and more "open" to you in my life. Amen.

CHAPTER 15

Towel and Soap: Create in Me a Clean Heart

MATERIALS AT HAND: A towel, soap of some kind, and a bowl of water for use as a basin, with a candle as a prayer focus.

CENTERING (Light the candle and say with your hands spread open:)

Loving God, Creator of all that is,
here I am—today, in this place,
with all the senses you have given me.
Help me to use them to experience you more deeply.
You are present everywhere around me;
open me to know more of the many ways
that your goodness surrounds me.
Thank you for this time to be with you and to listen to you.
Amen.

SAVORING:

Look at the towel, soap and water before you, noticing the differences in texture between the softness of the towel, the texture of the soap and the wetness of the water. Remember that what lies before you seems common and everyday in our culture but may not be as readily available to parts of the world's population.

Towel and Soap: Create in Me a Clean Heart

Smell the towel and soap to see if you notice any fragrance there, and try to predict what it will feel like to wash your hands in the water, using the soap. After you have imagined that with your senses, then slowly wash your hands with the soap and water, being aware of all your senses as you do.

Does it feel like you thought it would? What noises do you hear? How does the water look before and after your hands have been dipped in it? Take turns washing one hand with the other. When you are ready, dry your hands on the towel, savoring the softness and dryness of this piece of cloth that helps your hands go from wet to dry again.

What other similar experiences does this hand-washing bring to mind? Your regular bath or shower? Washing dishes? Bathing an infant or a pet? Washing the car? Even Baptism?

Now notice how your hands feel. Are they softer, perhaps wrinkled if you kept them in the water quite a while? Do they smell different? Is there a kind of newness to them that wasn't there before you washed them? This is such a simple action—washing one's hands—and yet not as ordinary as it might seem.

LISTENING:

Listen to one or more of these passages as you watch the candle play across the towel and soap:

Who shall ascend the hill of the LORD? And who shall stand in his holy place? Those who have clean hands and pure hearts, who do not lift up their souls to what is false, and do not swear deceitfully. They will receive blessing from the LORD, and vindication from the God of their salvation. (Ps 24:3–5)

Create in me a clean heart, O God, and put a new and right spirit within me. (Ps 51:10)

I will take you from the nations, and gather you from all the countries, and bring you into your own land. I will sprinkle clean water upon you, and you shall be clean from all your uncleannesses, and from all your idols I will cleanse you. A new heart I will give you, and a new spirit I will put within you; and I will remove from your body the heart of stone and give you a heart of flesh. (Ezek 36:24–26)

[Jesus] got up from the table, took off his outer robe, and tied a towel around himself. Then he poured water into a basin and began to wash the disciples' feet and to wipe them with the towel that was tied around him ... After he had washed their feet, had put on his robe, and had returned to the table, he said to them, "Do you know what I have done to you? You call me Teacher and Lord—and you are right, for that is what I am. So if I, your Lord and Teacher, have washed your feet, you also ought to wash one another's feet." (John 13:4–5, 12–14)

CONSIDERING:

Washing may happen somewhat differently in different cultures and different ages, but we know that it has been a practice since very early times. There is evidence of public bathing facilities from as early as 2000 BC, and the ancient Cretans and Egyptians, as well as the Greeks and Romans, seemed to have had public baths as a center of social life as well as a place for relaxation and recreation.

Social bathing has long been important in the Japanese culture, and we can also see it in the steam baths of Russia and Turkey or the dry heat of the Finnish sauna. Washing also has important significance for many religious traditions, such as the ritual washings of the Jewish tradition, baptism for Christians, washing in the Ganges river for Hindus, and even the Native American sweat lodge.

In the West, especially in the northern climates, bathing gradually became less common by the medieval era, and it really only became frequent again after the dirt and consequent disease of the Industrial Revolution required better hygiene. First the wealthy, and then the lower classes, gained the access to indoor means of bathing that we take for granted today.

Whether in the shower or soaking in a bathtub alone or enjoying a hot tub with friends, nothing refreshes and renews us quite like a bath.

Towel and Soap: Create in Me a Clean Heart

RESPONDING:

In two different references to bathing, Jesus warns his listeners—and us—about avoiding attitudes that can get in the way of our spiritual growth.

In yet another of his many blistering warnings to the Pharisees, who tended to be overly rigid in their religious interpretations, Jesus warns them about being too concerned about how others see them:

"Woe to you, scribes and Pharisees, hypocrites! For you clean the outside of the cup and of the plate, but inside . . . are full of greed and self-indulgence . . . First clean the inside of the cup, so that the outside also may become clean. Woe to you, scribes and Pharisees, hypocrites! For you are like whitewashed tombs, which on the outside look beautiful, but inside . . . are full of the bones of the dead and of all kinds of filth. So you also on the outside look righteous to others, but inside you are full of hypocrisy and lawlessness." (Matt 23:25–28)

Are *we* at times more concerned about how good and "clean" we look to others than what is really happening "on the inside?" Jesus reminds us here to first focus on our inner attitudes and feelings, and our actions will take care of themselves.

And in the midst of the washing of the feet passage mentioned in the Listening section above, Jesus also reminds us about the importance of balance in our lives through his conversation with Peter:

He came to Simon Peter, who said to him, "Lord, are you going to wash my feet?" Jesus answered, "You do not know now what I am doing, but later you will understand." Peter said to him, "You will never wash my feet." Jesus answered, "Unless I wash you, you have no share with me." Simon Peter said to him, "Lord, not my feet only but also my hands and my head!" Jesus said to him, "One who has bathed does not need to wash, except for the feet, but is entirely clean . . ." (John 13:6–10)

First, Peter refuses to let Jesus wash his feet at all—probably because he knew too well that *he* was the one who should be washing Jesus' feet, not vice-versa. Then Peter in his typical enthusiasm wants Jesus to wash him all over. Jesus seems to tell Peter—and us—to keep a good balance between the importance of being clean—doing what we know we need to do—but not *overdoing* it, either. Sometimes we can get so caught up in what we think is right that we become too rigid, like the Pharisees, or too busy to see God right before our eyes. Balance is important in our lives, whether it be about being clean, about helping others or trying to do too much, or even about religious practices.

In the Home and at School

      Loving God of soap and detergents, water and sponges and towels, bless all those who clean the places where we work and live. Bless those who make and sell cleaning equipment and supplies of all kinds. Bless, too, those without access to ways to clean themselves, their clothes and homes, especially refugees and the homeless. Bless those who care for, and bathe, those in hospitals and care facilities of various kinds.

      Help me to remember your cleansing and renewing care for me every time I wash my hands or take a bath or a shower. Amen.

CHAPTER 16

Pills or Medicine: The Gift of Health

MATERIALS AT HAND: Any medicine or pills, including vitamins, with a candle as a prayer focus.

CENTERING: (Light the candle and say with your hands spread open:)

Loving God, Creator of all that is,
here I am—today, in this place,
with all the senses you have given me.
Help me to use them to experience you more deeply.
You are present everywhere around me;
open me to know more of the many ways
that your goodness surrounds me.
Thank you for this time to be with you and to listen to you.
Amen.

SAVORING:

Look at the pills or other medicine before you, first considering the medicine in a general way, rather than for its specific purpose. Whether ointments, lotions, syrups, capsules, drops, tablets, powders, suppositories or tablets, the purpose of all medicines is to help our health and healing, a healing which we know ultimately comes from God.

Around the House

Consider now the specific form of the vitamins or medicine before you. Notice the texture and shape, color and size of it, holding either the medicine or its container in your hand. Think about what it was meant to help with and how many more problems there might be if it didn't exist.

Reflect on all the work that has gone into the production of this substance. What you see before you is the fruit of many years of research and testing to try to find the best ways to help our bodies heal and to keep them healthy. There are so many kinds of people throughout history that would regard what lies before you as magic or as a miracle—which, in a sense, it is. This is an example of the fruit of God's gift of intelligence to us as humans, an intelligence which has helped us discover and understand what can aid the body in its remarkable process of healing.

Think of all the ways that you have been helped back to health and all the other people throughout the world who have been helped by such amazing discoveries. Such mighty wonders in such a small package, and so easy to take for granted!

LISTENING:

Listen to one or more of these passages as you watch the candle play across the medicine or vitamins:

A cheerful heart is a good medicine, but a downcast spirit dries up the bones. (Prov 17:22)

Honor physicians for their services, for the Lord created them; for their gift of healing comes from the Most High . . . The skill of physicians makes them distinguished, and in the presence of the great they are admired. The Lord created medicines out of the earth, and the sensible will not despise them . . . And he gave skill to human beings that he might be glorified in his marvelous works. By them the physician heals and takes away pain; the pharmacist makes a mixture from them. God's works will never be finished; and from him health spreads over all the earth. My child, when you are ill, do not delay, but pray to the Lord, and he will heal you. (Sira 38:1–4, 6–9)

Faithful friends are life-saving medicine; and those who fear the Lord will find them. (Sir 6:16)

Pills or Medicine: The Gift of Health

Raphael said to Tobias, before he had approached his father [Tobit], "I know that his eyes will be opened. Smear the gall of the fish on his eyes; the medicine will make the white films shrink and peel off from his eyes, and your father will regain his sight and see the light." . . . Then Tobit got up and came stumbling out through the courtyard door. Tobias went up to him, with the gall of the fish in his hand, and holding him firmly, he blew into his eyes, saying, "Take courage, father." With this he applied the medicine on his eyes, and it made them smart. Next, with both his hands he peeled off the white films from the corners of his eyes. Then Tobit saw his son and threw his arms around him, and he wept and said to him, "I see you, my son, the light of my eyes!" Then he said, "Blessed be God, and blessed be his great name, and blessed be all his holy angels. May his holy name be blessed throughout all the ages. Though he afflicted me, he has had mercy upon me. Now I see my son Tobias!" So Tobit went in rejoicing and praising God at the top of his voice. (Tob 11:7–8,10–15)

As [Jesus] walked along, he saw a man blind from birth . . . [and] he spat on the ground and made mud with the saliva and spread the mud on the man's eyes, saying to him, "Go, wash in the pool of Siloam" (which means Sent). Then he went and washed and came back able to see. (John 9:1,6–7)

[Jesus said to his disciples,] "Whenever you enter a town and its people welcome you, eat what is set before you; cure the sick who are there, and say to them, 'The kingdom of God has come near to you.'" (Luke 10:8–9)

CONSIDERING:

Our modern medicines are the product of a long and uneven history. In ancient times people either thought that the illness came from demons, so that it needed to be driven out of the body, or else the immediate wound or problem was treated directly, by means that often included plant extracts. Some of those plant extracts—like digitalis from foxglove to help stimulate the heart—are still used today.

Many ancient civilizations had important insights into the treatment of illnesses, but some did not allow dissection of human corpses, which limited their knowledge of basic biology and the effects of disease. By the sixth century BC the ancient Greeks no longer saw illness as a punishment from the gods, as it had been considered earlier. They gradually focused more on preventive methods, which the Romans also helped improve by their emphasis on public health.

By the Middle Ages, however, much of the early Greek and Roman contributions had been lost, due to the barbarian invasions, and much of health care was a matter of folklore and magic. This was only ended when the Arabic culture rediscovered and revived ancient Greek and Roman medicine, which had also been partially preserved in the monasteries of Europe during the medieval period.

Modern medicine really began in the seventeenth century when the circulation of the blood was discovered, and the nineteenth century saw the development of important tools such as the modern stethoscope. Researchers such as Pasteur and Koch in the field of bacteriology have helped us understand the existence of germs and the need for antibiotics and vaccines, and more recent medical research has helped us understand far more about viruses, hormones and vitamins and be able to develop the medicines to use this knowledge for better health.

RESPONDING:

Healing and health is still a mysterious process to us, even as we know far more than we used to about how our bodies work and about how to help them regain health holistically. For example, recent research has shown that praying for those who are recovering can have a measurable physical effect on patients—even if they do not know they are being prayed for. Are there people that I know who could use my prayer support as they try to recover their health? Can I visit or call or drop a note to someone who needs the healing support and "medicine" that I can give right now to try improve his or her health?

In general, am I "good medicine" to those around me, a positive presence who appreciates others and lets them know how much I value them? Are there some specific ways that I can plan to let some of the people in my life know how they are a blessing to me?

Do I use well what I put into my body, not abusing tobacco or alcohol or other drugs and appropriately using medicines and vitamins that can help my health—neither overusing them or refusing to use them when warranted?

Loving God of tablets and capsules, shots and x-rays, of surgery and prescriptions, bless all those who help us keep and regain our health,

Pills or Medicine: The Gift of Health

from doctors to pharmacists to all those studying these fields. Bless the researchers and producers of medicines and vitamins; help them to make these important tools with care and to charge a just amount for them.

Please bless all those whose health depends on medications for their survival and health, and be with those who need such medicines and do not have access to them, especially the many throughout the world dying from HIV and AIDS. And bless those working for a just availability of medical resources.

Help me to remember whenever I see a bottle of medicine that you are our true Healer, and that your "prescription" for each one of us is your gentle, tender love. Amen.

CHAPTER 17

Newspaper: Believe in the Good News

Materials at hand: A newspaper, folded so that no particular story is prominent, and a candle as a prayer focus.

CENTERING: (Light the candle and say with your hands spread open:)

Loving God, Creator of all that is,
here I am—today, in this place,
with all the senses you have given me.
Help me to use them to experience you more deeply.
You are present everywhere around me;
open me to know more of the many ways
that your goodness surrounds me.
Thank you for this time to be with you and to listen to you.
Amen.

SAVORING:

Look at the paper folded before you, at all the black—or colored—marks on the newsprint. Imagine for a moment that the newspaper is printed in a different language. What would the letters look like then?

Imagine, too, some headlines you might prefer to read over the ones that are actually there: "Nations of the World Conclude Agreement on World Peace," "Last Homeless Person Given a Place to Live." What else

Newspaper: Believe in the Good News

would you like to read? That you won the lottery? That the cure for the last major disease in the world had been found? What's the best news you can think of to read?

Slowly unfold the paper, listening for the sound it makes and feeling the texture of the paper as you do. Think of all the people all over the world doing this at various times today. Think, too, of the many kinds of ways that people's lives are recorded in these pages around the world: births and deaths, world and local events, sports and business and much more.

While not our only source in this age of many types of media, newspapers provide an important source for the information we hunger for every day, the news of what is happening around us

LISTENING:

Listen to one or more of these passages as you watch the candle play across the newspaper:

. . . the angel said to [the shepherds], "Do not be afraid; for see—I am bringing you good news of great joy for all the people: to you is born this day in the city of David a Savior, who is the Messiah, the Lord. This will be a sign for you: you will find a child wrapped in bands of cloth and lying in a manger." (Luke 2:10–12)

How beautiful upon the mountains are the feet of the messenger who announces peace, who brings good news, who announces salvation, who says to Zion, "your God reigns." (Is 52:7)

Now after John was arrested, Jesus came to Galilee, proclaiming the good news of God, and saying, "The time is fulfilled, and the kingdom of God has come near; repent, and believe in the good news." (Mark 1:14–15)

The light of the eyes rejoices the heart, and good news refreshes the body. (Prov 15:30)

Around the House

CONSIDERING:

Newspapers—whether daily or weekly, domestic or foreign—help us to make sense out of what happens in our world. And we read them more than one might think in this multi-media age. In this country, for example, about 1700 daily papers print a total of about 63 million copies, and almost every copy is read by at least two people. There are also 6800 weekly newspapers, each with a healthy circulation. Publishers estimate that nearly 8 out of 10 Americans read a newspaper daily. Newspapers are also an important force in other parts of the world, although some governments are not as intentional about the freedom of the press as is the United States.

But newspapers are a fairly recent way to receive the news. Until the early to mid-seventeenth century, information happened mainly by word of mouth. But then, thanks to moveable metal type, papers which looked more like what we would call newsletters began to appear in parts of Europe. It was the early eighteenth century before they appeared in what would become the United States, and it's no coincidence that newspaper publishers like Benjamin Franklin would have a big impact on the revolutionary movement when it happened in "the Colonies."

Newspapers around the world not only report the news, but in a very real sense they help shape the news as the editors make countless decisions every day and week about what constitutes "news" or not, as do others involved in other news media.

In Jesus' time the only source of news was oral communication, and the good news—or "gospel"—that he came to share was first an oral message before it later became written down.

Whether "good news" or bad, the information we gain from newspapers and other sources is essential in helping us understand the world in which we live.

RESPONDING:

The book of Proverbs observes, "Like cold water to a thirsty soul, so is good news from a far country." (Prov 25:25)

If God's love for us *is* good news, as Jesus came to show us, do we really see our faith as good news, like the fact that a friend came through cancer surgery or treatment successfully or that our team won the game?

Newspaper: Believe in the Good News

Or do we just take that faith in God's love so for granted that it no longer seems all that "new" or "good"?

And in our own lives, do we tend to focus on the "good news," the positive events and developments that happen, or do we focus on the "bad news," the people who have let us down or our own disappointments or discontent? Is our proverbial glass half empty or half full as we look at our lives? Dear God, help me to see the wonder of your love and the gifts and grace in my life more clearly than I have in the past.

This good news of God's love is not intended for us to keep it to ourselves. In Mark's gospel Jesus says to his apostles—and to us: ". . . Go into all the world and proclaim the good news to the whole creation . . . And they went out and proclaimed the good news everywhere, while the Lord worked with them and confirmed the message by the signs that accompanied it." (Mark 16:15, 20)

Each of us is called to "spread the word" in a different fashion, according to our gifts and interests and unique personality. There are as many ways to proclaim the good news as there are people on the earth.

How am *I* called to share the good news with those around me? s it through being a caring and peaceful presence to those around me at work and home? Is it through being more involved in my local church? Or what? A quote often attributed to St. Francis of Assisi puts it well: "Preach the Gospel at all times; if necessary use words."

Loving God of all forms of information and news, bless all those who work on newspapers and other forms of news media, online and off, including editors, reporters, photographers and so many people behind the scenes. Bless, too, those in the headlines today and also those whose news is important but who may have been ignored by the news sources.

Help me to appreciate more fully the good news of your limitless love for me when I see a newspaper or watch or listen to the news. Amen.

CHAPTER 18

Clothing: Put On Love

Materials at hand: A couple pieces of clothing, and a candle as a prayer focus.

CENTERING (Light the candle and say with your hands spread open:)

Loving God, Creator of all that is,
here I am—today, in this place,
with all the senses you have given me.
Help me to use them to experience you more deeply.
You are present everywhere around me;
open me to know more of the many ways
that your goodness surrounds me.
Thank you for this time to be with you and to listen to you.
Amen.

SAVORING:

As you look at the pieces of clothing before you, pretend that you don't recognize them and have never seen them before. Notice what you can about them visually before using your other senses. What colors are they? What textures and fabrics do you see before you? Are the fabrics rough or smooth, soft or bumpy like corduroy? Do you notice any buttons or zippers or snaps as the clothes lie before you? Any collars or decorations?

Clothing: Put On Love

Now use your fingers to explore what you have seen, closing your eyes to focus better on one sense. Experience the textures and details, not trying to identify which garment you are touching or where. Does your nose or do your ears give you any further information, still keeping your eyes closed? Is there a distinctive smell or any noise associated with the garments you might not have noticed before? If someone from a different culture or even a different planet were to come across these garments, do you think that person would they know what they were for?

Now, think back to when these pieces of clothing were constructed, starting out perhaps as a bolt of cloth and before that some yarn, thread or fiber of some sort. Consider all the processes they needed to go through to make it to you, from being woven or knitted to being cut out and sewn to being shipped to a store and then bought by you—or perhaps made by you at home. Think, too, of the number of times these garments have been worn since they were new, all the days and all the ways that they have covered you and kept you comfortable and protected.

While holding these clothes before you, consider also the ones you are wearing now. "Check in" with your skin at various places throughout your body and see how the clothing feels against it. Does your body feel comfortable and carefully surrounded or are there places where your clothing irritates or binds in any way? Be thankful for the gift of clothing that covers and shelters you.

LISTENING:

Listen to one or more of these passages as you watch the candle play across the clothing:

So when the woman saw that the tree [in the garden] was good for food, and that it was a delight to the eyes, and that the tree was to be desired to make one wise, she took of its fruit and ate; and she also gave some to her husband, who was with her, and he ate. Then the eyes of both were opened, and they knew that they were naked; and they sewed fig leaves together and made loincloths for themselves. (Gen 3:6–7)

[John the Baptist] went into all the region around the Jordan, proclaiming a baptism of repentance for the forgiveness of sins . . . And the crowds asked him, "What then should we do?" In reply he said to them, "Whoever

Around the House

has two coats must share with anyone who has none; and whoever has food must do likewise." (Luke 3:3,10–11)

Now there was a woman who had been suffering from hemorrhages for twelve years . . . She had heard about Jesus, and came up behind him in the crowd and touched his cloak, for she said, "If I but touch his clothes, I will be made well." Immediately her hemorrhage stopped; and she felt in her body that she was healed of her disease.

Immediately aware that power had gone forth from him, Jesus turned about in the crowd and said, "Who touched my clothes?" And his disciples said to him, "You see the crowd pressing in on you; how can you say, 'Who touched me?'" He looked all around to see who had done it. But the woman, knowing what had happened to her, came in fear and trembling, fell down before him, and told him the whole truth. He said to her, "Daughter, your faith has made you well; go in peace, and be healed of your disease." (Mark 5:25, 27–34)

[Then the king will say to those on his right hand,] I was naked and you gave me clothing, I was sick and you took care of me, I was in prison and you visited me.' Then the righteous will answer him, 'Lord, when was it that we saw you hungry and gave you food, or thirsty and gave you something to drink? And when was it that we saw you a stranger and welcomed you, or naked and gave you clothing? . . . And the king will answer them, 'Truly I tell you, just as you did it to one of the least of these who are members of my family, you did it to me.' (Mat t25:36–38, 40)

When the soldiers had crucified Jesus, they took his clothes and divided them into four parts, one for each soldier. They also took his tunic; now the tunic was seamless, woven in one piece from the top. So they said to one another, "Let us not tear it, but cast lots for it to see who will get it." This was to fulfill what the scripture says, "They divided my clothes among themselves, and for my clothing they cast lots." (John 19:23–24)

. . . [C]an any of you by worrying add a single hour to your span of life? If then you are not able to do so small a thing as that, why do you worry about the rest? Consider the lilies, how they grow: they neither toil nor spin; yet I tell you, even Solomon in all his glory was not clothed like one of these. But if God so clothes the grass of the field, which is alive today

Clothing: Put On Love

and tomorrow is thrown into the oven, how much more will he clothe you—you of little faith! (Luke 12:25-28)

CONSIDERING:

Clothing serves many different purposes for us. Besides protecting us from the climate in which we live, it also serves as a way for us to express ourselves in terms of fashion and particular tastes, especially in Western cultures. In general, people living in warmer climates have developed looser- fitting garments of light colored cloth to help protect them from the sun, while the inhabitants of colder environments have developed more close-fitting and heavier garments to help keep in their own body heat and protect against the cold.

The earliest clothing was probably made from animal skins. We know that in the ancient Middle East generally men and women wore a loose tunic, with or without sleeves, that could be tucked up if needed while working, and they wore a cloak when needed over that for warmth. In addition, women generally wore veils to cover their heads.

Gradually, through the centuries with increased trade the various world cultures were exposed to new fabrics and new fashions and designs. And now with the advent of synthetic fabrics—mainly in the twentieth century—we have many options of fabrics, colors and style from which that we can choose, for everything from the heaviest coat to the lightest swimsuit.

RESPONDING:

When it comes to clothing, scripture can help remind us to not judge by appearances and also to watch what qualities we "wear."

In the letter of James, the author reminds the community to whom he is writing that although it's tempting to size people up by what they are wearing and treat them accordingly, it's not being faithful to the way Jesus treated others:

My brothers and sisters, do you with your acts of favoritism really believe in our glorious Lord Jesus Christ? For if a person with gold rings and in fine clothes comes into your assembly, and if a poor person in dirty clothes also comes in, and if you take notice of the one wearing the fine clothes and say, "Have a seat here, please," while to the one who is poor you say, "Stand there," or, "Sit at my feet," have you not made distinctions among yourselves, and become judges with evil thoughts? Listen, my beloved brothers and sisters. Has not God chosen the poor in the world to be rich in faith and to be heirs of the kingdom that he has promised to those who love him? (James 2:1–5)

How often am I aware of how others are dressed and make a judgment based on that observation? Probably more often than I realize. I will try to make it a point to not pass judgment based on appearance alone.

In the letter to the Christians at Colossus, Paul uses the image of clothing to suggest the virtues they needed to work on acquiring. Listen to his excellent list:

As God's chosen ones, holy and beloved, clothe yourselves with compassion, kindness, humility, meekness, and patience. Bear with one another and, if anyone has a complaint against another, forgive each other; just as the Lord has forgiven you, so you also must forgive. Above all, clothe yourselves with love, which binds everything together in perfect harmony. (Col 3:12–14)

Which of these qualities do you think you do the best at "wearing?" Which is the hardest for you to "put on?" Pick one of these to try to work on for the next few days. And also take a look in your closets and drawers for any unused clothing and give it away to someone else or to a group who will share it with those who need it.

Loving God of looms and knitting needles, of satin and denim, of jackets and socks, thank you for the gift of clothing and all the ways that we can express ourselves with it as well as protect our bodies. Bless those who make clothing, especially those who work under unsafe or unfair conditions in sweatshops and those who are helping to change those conditions. Bless, too, those who design and sell clothes; help them to use their gifts well and fairly.

Please bless those without enough to wear or an ability to keep warm enough; help us to be aware of them and share what we have more freely and generously.

Thank you for the gift of clothing, and please help me to "put on love" and to remember that you are closer to me than my clothing when I'm getting dressed each day. Amen.

CHAPTER 19

Hammer and Nails: A Time to Build

Materials at hand: A hammer, a few nails and a piece of wood, with a candle as a prayer focus.

CENTERING (Light the candle and say with your hands spread open:)

Loving God, Creator of all that is,
here I am—today, in this place,
with all the senses you have given me.
Help me to use them to experience you more deeply.
You are present everywhere around me;
open me to know more of the many ways
that your goodness surrounds me.
Thank you for this time to be with you and to listen to you.
Amen.

SAVORING:

As you consider the hammer and nails before you, notice the care with which they are made. The hammer is designed to do one main job and was built with that in mind. Think of all the times this hammer has been used and what it may have helped build. Consider, too, all the hammers throughout history that have helped construct buildings of all kinds in many parts of the world.

Around the House

Listen in your imagination to the sound of the hammer on the nail, pounding and driving it where it needs to go. Predict how the hammer will feel in your hand, based on the times you have used it before. What were you using it for then? Now feel the hammer, its weight and its strength, and feel the potential for either building or destroying, whether using the head of the hammer or its claw. Swing it to get a sense of the power it can hold.

The nails before you are all uniform so that they can all do the same work and are designed to go in smoothly and hold firmly. However, nails were not so always so uniform when they were made by hand in the past. Hold one of the nails and imagine the way it must "feel" as the nail enters the wood and pushes its way in between the grain in the wood. Carefully feel the surface and the grain of the wood, imagining where this piece of lumber was when it was still growing and alive.

Here before you are the elements of building, an activity that happens around us countless times every day.

LISTENING:

Listen to one or more of these passages as you watch the candle play across the hammer, nails and wood:

For everything there is a season, and a time for every matter under heaven: . . . a time to break down, and a time to build up . . . (Eccl 3:1,3)

Now when [King David] was settled in his house, and the LORD had given him rest from all his enemies around him, the king said to the prophet Nathan, "See now, I am living in a house of cedar, but the ark of God stays in a tent." . . . But that same night the word of the LORD came to Nathan: Go and tell my servant David: Thus says the LORD: Are you the one to build me a house to live in? I have not lived in a house since the day I brought up the people of Israel from Egypt to this day, but I have been moving about in a tent and a tabernacle. Wherever I have moved about among all the people of Israel, did I ever speak a word with any of the tribal leaders of Israel, whom I commanded to shepherd my people Israel, saying, "Why have you not built me a house of cedar?" . . . the LORD declares to you that the LORD will make you a house. When your days are fulfilled and you lie down with your ancestors, I will raise up your offspring after you, who shall come forth from your body, and I

Hammer and Nails: A Time to Build

will establish his kingdom. He shall build a house for my name, and I will establish the throne of his kingdom forever. (2 Sam 7:1–2, 4–7, 11–13)

Unless the LORD builds the house, those who build it labor in vain. (Ps 127:1)

On the sabbath he began to teach in the synagogue, and many who heard him were astounded. They said, "Where did this man get all this? What is this wisdom that has been given to him? What deeds of power are being done by his hands! Is not this the carpenter, the son of Mary and brother of James and Joses and Judas and Simon, and are not his sisters here with us?" (Mark 6:2–3)

"Why do you call me 'Lord, Lord,' and do not do what I tell you? I will show you what someone is like who comes to me, hears my words, and acts on them. That one is like a man building a house, who dug deeply and laid the foundation on rock; when a flood arose, the river burst against that house but could not shake it, because it had been well built. But the one who hears and does not act is like a man who built a house on the ground without a foundation. When the river burst against it, immediately it fell, and great was the ruin of that house." (Luke 6:46–49)

For we are God's servants, working together; you are . . . God's building. According to the grace of God given to me, like a skilled master builder I laid a foundation, and someone else is building on it. Each builder must choose with care how to build on it. For no one can lay any foundation other than the one that has been laid; that foundation is Jesus Christ . . . Do you not know that you are God's temple and that God's Spirit dwells in you? (1 Cor 3:9–11, 16)

CONSIDERING:

There are an amazing variety of buildings in our world, from tents to temples, pyramids to pagodas, houses to huts, barns to basilicas, castles to cottages, log cabins, igloos, monuments and tombs and everything in between. Besides wood, the materials that are used range from clay, sod, and stucco to bricks, sticks, hay bales and even reeds, from glass, steel and concrete to tile. Some of the variables that will affect a building's appearance include the style that is locally popular, the climate, available materials, local know-how, its purpose, and the social and economic status of the one having the structure built.

It is easy for those in our culture to assume that a building to be used as a home would usually be built to accommodate a single family, with a number of rooms, areas for storage, as well as certain elements that we can take for granted, such as heating, running water and one or more indoor toilets. However, when we stop to think about it, none of these elements was a given in the past—nor is it at times in the present.

There are many inventions that have affected our buildings in countless ways. For example, it is really only after the elevator became widely available after the Civil War that we have the development of taller apartment houses and buildings for business, leading to our present skyscrapers.

For all the variety that exists, there are certain common elements shared by the most humble and the most elaborate buildings, from a floor—and usually a foundation—to walls, windows, doors and a roof of some kind. Whether complex or simple, there is so much to a building that we can so easily take for granted.

RESPONDING:

The image of a building appears a number of times in scripture to help challenge us as to what we are "building" with our lives. For example, Jesus reminds us that life is not just about having more and more:

And he said to them, "Take care! Be on your guard against all kinds of greed; for one's life does not consist in the abundance of possessions." Then he told them a parable: "The land of a rich man produced abundantly. And he thought to himself, 'What should I do, for I have no place to store my crops?' Then he said, 'I will do this: I will pull down my barns and build larger ones, and there I will store all my grain and my goods. And I will say to my soul, Soul, you have ample goods laid up for many years; relax, eat, drink, be merry.' But God said to him, 'You fool! This very night your life is being demanded of you. And the things you have prepared, whose will they be?' So it is with those who store up treasures for themselves but are not rich toward God." (Luke 12:15-21)

The prophet Jeremiah also reminds us how important it is that justice to others be one of the "materials" used in building our lives. "Woe to him who builds his house by unrighteousness, and his upper rooms by

Hammer and Nails: A Time to Build

injustice; who makes his neighbors work for nothing, and does not give them their wages . . . " (Jer 22:13) What am *I* building with my life so far, and how much does justice to others, both those I know and those I may never meet, play a role in that "structure?"

What is the" foundation" for my life? Is it my faith—or do I just *say* that it is? If faith really is my foundation, do I realize that it may cost me something in my life to be a Christian? At another point in Luke's gospel Jesus challenges his listeners—and us—not to "underestimate" the challenges that following him will mean:

Now large crowds were traveling with [Jesus]; and he turned and said to them, "Whoever comes to me and does not hate father and mother, wife and children, brothers and sisters, yes, and even life itself, cannot be my disciple. Whoever does not carry the cross and follow me cannot be my disciple. For which of you, intending to build a tower, does not first sit down and estimate the cost, to see whether he has enough to complete it? Otherwise, when he has laid a foundation and is not able to finish, all who see it will begin to ridicule him, saying, 'This fellow began to build and was not able to finish.' (Luke 14:25-30)

At this point in the "building" of my life, are there some "timbers" that aren't quite straight or some "bent nails" that need to be removed and replaced with straighter ones? Is everything in my life helping me build to where I want to go, or are there parts of my life that are getting in the way that need to be changed or set aside? Maybe those are attitudes or habits or perhaps friends that aren't helping me grow and "build" in the way I'd like to in my life. Please give me the grace to take a look at those areas and the courage to change them if I need to.

If I keep trying to live in faith, my faith will continue to build, as we are reminded in the letter to Jude: "But you, beloved, build yourselves up in your most holy faith; pray in the Holy Spirit; keep yourselves in the love of God; look forward to the mercy of our Lord Jesus Christ that leads to eternal life." (Jude 1:20-21)

Loving God of hovels and high-rises, bless all those who help make the buildings we use and enjoy, from architects and engineers to contractors, carpenters, plumbers, electricians, framers and roofers. Bless all those without a place to live, because of financial reasons or through natural disasters or war. Bless all who work with organizations like Habitat for Humanity to help to "build" a better world. And when I see a building, help me to examine what kind of a life I am "constructing" with your help. Amen.

CHAPTER 20

Bandage: You Have Healed Me

Materials at hand: A few packaged bandages or some gauze and tape, with a candle as a prayer focus.

CENTERING (Light the candle and say with your hands spread open:)

Loving God, Creator of all that is,
here I am—today, in this place,
with all the senses you have given me.
Help me to use them to experience you more deeply.
You are present everywhere around me;
open me to know more of the many ways
that your goodness surrounds me.
Thank you for this time to be with you and to listen to you.
Amen.

SAVORING:

Look at the bandages (or the material for them) before you. Think of all the times you have gotten hurt and needed one of these, perhaps especially as a child, and how someone helped you when you needed it. Consider, too, all the people who may be injured in various parts of the world—whether through war or just daily accidents—who may not have access to the health care we too often take for granted.

Bandage: You Have Healed Me

Now touch the bandaging supplies before you, after predicting what your fingers will experience. Feel the various textures involved, from the stickiness of the tape or adhesive strip to the softness of the gauze or the pad on the adhesive strip. Listen to the noise that the wrappers may make, wrappers that are there to keep the bandages clean and sterile till needed. If you can spare it, open an adhesive strip and slowly put it on your skin, experiencing it as though for the first time.

As you look at the bandages before you, take some time to consider also the many ways in which you have been hurt *inside*, wounds that don't show on the outside or leave a visible scar and therefore are more subtle. Maybe those wounds involve how you have been treated or spoken to or regarded by others; perhaps they include your disappointments with others as they fell short of what you expected of them. Then consider how this inner wounding has happened for others as well.

Whether the "owies" are on the outside and visible, needing a bandage or on the inside where they can't be seen, healing them can take a long time.

LISTENING:

Listen to one or more of these passages as you watch the candle play across the bandages:

For thus says the LORD: your hurt is incurable, your wound is grievous ... [But] I will restore health to you, and your wounds I will heal, says the LORD ... (Jer 30:12, 17)

The LORD builds up Jerusalem; he gathers the outcasts of Israel. He heals the brokenhearted, and binds up their wounds. (Ps 147:2–3)

Jesus replied, "A man was going down from Jerusalem to Jericho, and fell into the hands of robbers, who stripped him, beat him, and went away, leaving him half dead. Now by chance a priest was going down that road; and when he saw him, he passed by on the other side. So likewise a Levite, when he came to the place and saw him, passed by on the other side. But a Samaritan while traveling came near him; and when he saw him, he was moved with pity. He went to him and bandaged his wounds, having poured oil and wine on them. Then he put him on his own animal, brought him to an inn, and took care of him. The next day he took out two denarii, gave them to the innkeeper, and said, 'Take care of him; and when I come back, I will repay you whatever more you spend.' Which of these three, do you think, was a neighbor to the man who fell into the hands of the robbers?" He said, "The one who showed him mercy." Jesus said to him, "Go and do likewise." (Luke 10:30–37)

[Jesus] himself bore our sins in his body on the cross, so that, free from sins, we might live for righteousness; by his wounds you have been healed. (1 Pet 2:24)

And wherever he went, into villages or cities or farms, they laid the sick in the marketplaces, and begged him that they might touch even the fringe of his cloak; and all who touched it were healed. (Mark 6:56)

O LORD my God, I cried to you for help, and you have healed me. (Ps 30:2)

CONSIDERING:

The way the body heals is nothing less than amazing. When we cover a wound with a bandage, we are just protecting it while the body does the healing. Somehow it knows just what is needed to heal what was injured and return to full health again. As a wound begins to heal, it does so through what scientists call granulation, and the body forms the fibrous tissue that we later call a scar. The potential complications in this healing process are too great a loss of blood or a possible infection; thus the need for a bandage.

Before modern medical knowledge people often relied on folk remedies to promote healing. For example, in Europe and America in the seventeenth and eighteenth centuries cobwebs from the cellar spider were often used as bandages to help stop bleeding from wounds, and many medicines were based on herbs and plants.

Jesus certainly knew about healing; wherever he went he healed the sick as a sign of the fuller spiritual healing and love that he had come to announce, and people flocked to him for that healing presence. Just like those who sought him out, we all long for healing in our lives, whether we know it or not.

Bandage: You Have Healed Me

RESPONDING:

The book of Ecclesiastes tells us, "For everything there is a season, and a time for every matter under heaven: . . . a time to heal; a time to break down, and a time to build up; . . . a time to seek, and a time to lose; a time to keep, and a time to throw away;" (Eccl 3:1,3,6) Is this a time to heal in my life, and if so from what? Are there any old "wounds" that I haven't let go of which keep getting in the way of my ability to fully enjoy my life and the freedom of God's love? Healing God, please help me forgive all those who may have hurt either me or others around me and help me to feel your healing love.

Bless all those who are sick, especially those whose conditions are life-threatening; bless those who help care for the sick or wounded and those who make the bandages and all the supplies needed to care for them. Please bless and help heal those who suffer from "wounds" that may not be visible, especially from all kinds of abuse and from Post-Traumatic Stress Disorder (PTSD). And please help us understand better how to "heal" the problems between countries and groups through tools like mediation and reconciliation.

God of Love, thank you for your healing love; help me remember it whenever I see a bandage. Amen.

CHAPTER 21

Needle and Thread: A Time to Sew

Materials at hand: A spool of thread and needle, a piece of fabric or some yarn and knitting needles, with a candle as a prayer focus.

CENTERING (Light the candle and say with your hands spread open:)

Loving God, Creator of all that is,
here I am—today, in this place,
with all the senses you have given me.
Help me to use them to experience you more deeply.
You are present everywhere around me;
open me to know more of the many ways
that your goodness surrounds me.
Thank you for this time to be with you and to listen to you.
Amen.

SAVORING:

Take a look at the tools and material before you, for that's what they are. Think of the potential they have for creating clothing or costumes or other coverings or decorations. Notice the colors and the textures involved—the smooth, sharp needle and the smooth sheen of the thread, the texture of the fabric and its folds in the candle's light or the soft warmth of the yarn.

Needle and Thread: A Time to Sew

Before touching the various materials before you, try to predict what your fingers will experience. Then, while exploring them with your fingers, try to close your eyes so that you can concentrate on what your fingers are telling you.

If you have sewn or knitted, do your hands have memories of what they have done before with similar resources? If so, recall what that process was like and the satisfaction of going from "raw materials" of one sort to a finished product that could be used in some way. Whether or not you have sewn before, if you could make anything with your fingers, what would it be and how would it look? Are the clothes you are wearing now woven or knitted or a combination of both? Imagine the processes that led to their present form.

Whether or not you're a sewer, knitter or weaver, be thankful for the gift of coordination in our fingers through which we are able to do complex tasks like weaving, sewing and knitting and even devise machines that can do much of that job for us.

LISTENING:

Listen to one or more of these passages as you watch the candle play across the needle, thread and fabric or yarn:

For everything there is a season, and a time for every matter under heaven . . . a time to tear, and a time to sew . . . (Eccl 3:1,7)

And [Mary] gave birth to her firstborn son and wrapped him in bands of cloth, and laid him in a manger, because there was no place for them in the inn . . . (Luke 2:7)

Now there was a good and righteous man named Joseph, who . . . came from the Jewish town of Arimathea, and he was waiting expectantly for the kingdom of God. This man went to Pilate and asked for the body of Jesus. Then he took it down, wrapped it in a linen cloth, and laid it in a rock-hewn tomb where no one had ever been laid. (Luke 23:50–53)

Jesus said to them again, "Children, how hard it is to enter the kingdom of God! It is easier for a camel to go through the eye of a needle than for someone who is rich to enter the kingdom of God." They were greatly astounded and said to one another, "Then who can be saved?" Jesus looked at them and said, "For mortals it is impossible, but not for God; for God all things are possible." (Mark 10:24-27)

When the soldiers had crucified Jesus, they took his clothes and divided them into four parts, one for each soldier. They also took his tunic; now the tunic was seamless, woven in one piece from the top. So they said to one another, "Let us not tear it, but cast lots for it to see who will get it." This was to fulfill what the scripture says, "They divided my clothes among themselves, and for my clothing they cast lots." (John 19:23-24)

CONSIDERING:

Spinning, weaving and sewing are topics we don't give much thought to usually—unless they happen to be hobbies of ours—because of the manufactured fabric around us. But for much of the world's history, and for some peoples today, the only way fabrics and garments existed was through hand weaving and sewing.

Today textiles may come from the farm—those of cotton, wool, silk or flax—or from the chemist—fabrics of rayon, nylon, and polyesters such as dacron and acrylic. These raw materials are spun into yarns and then made into fabric by weaving or knitting them together, usually in mills where the whole process is coordinated and controlled by computers and very few people are involved. Then, after dyeing and finishing, the fabric will go to a retailer or to a manufacturer of textile products.

Besides being used for clothing, fabric is a part of our lives in other ways, such as upholstery and draperies or curtains. Textiles are "sew" important and yet can be easily taken for granted in our lives.

RESPONDING:

The image of the weaving and knitting of fabrics appears in some interesting places in scripture to remind us about key aspects of our lives.

The Psalmist, for example, reminds us that we owe our very existence to God's loving care and attention. "O LORD, you have searched me and known me. . . . For it was you who formed my inward parts; you knit me together in my mother's womb. I praise you, for I am fearfully and wonderfully made." (Ps 139:1,13-24) Have you thought about the wonder

Needle and Thread: A Time to Sew

of your very existence lately and the amazing way all the systems within your body work together so intricately and so well?

The prophet Isaiah describes how king Hezekiah, after recovering from a mortal illness, feared that the "weaving" of his life was over and "folded up"—until he was saved:

> I said, I shall not see the LORD in the land of the living; I shall look upon mortals no more among the inhabitants of the world. My dwelling is plucked up and removed from me like a shepherd's tent; like a weaver I have rolled up my life; he cuts me off from the loom ... (Is 38:11–12)

If you think of *your* life as a piece of fabric, a weaving laid out on a loom, what have been the main "colors" and themes so far? Is that what you want to continue or are there some other "threads" you'd like to highlight or bring into the "weave?" If so, what are they?

One of the images Jesus used when asked why his teaching and way of life was so different from that of other religious teachers of the time was that of a piece of fabric:

> Then the disciples of John came to [Jesus] saying, "Why do we and the Pharisees fast often, but your disciples do not fast?" And Jesus said to them, "The wedding guests cannot mourn as long as the bridegroom is with them, can they? The days will come when the bridegroom is taken away from them, and then they will fast. No one sews a piece of unshrunk cloth on an old cloak, for the patch pulls away from the cloak, and a worse tear is made." (Matt 9:14–16)

Jesus is telling his listeners—and us—that He's doing something different than the way religion has been seen till then. How well do you appreciate the ways that really following Jesus can mean "tearing away" from the comfortable way you may have seen life and going in some new and unexpected directions at times? Are you willing to listen for the challenge of the gospel message, even if it makes you somewhat uncomfortable?

Loving God of the spindle, loom, cutting table and needle, bless those who sew, knit, crochet, embroider, quilt and in many ways help make our clothing and our lives more attractive. Bless those who weave fabrics and rugs throughout the world. Bless seamstresses, tailors, garment workers, upholsterers and all those who work with fabrics in any way.

Help me to think of the ways your love is woven around me and within me whenever I see a piece of fabric. Amen.

All Around Us

CHAPTER 22

A Leaf or Branch: Alive in Christ

MATERIALS AT HAND: A leaf or branch of any kind, with a candle as a prayer focus.

CENTERING (Light the candle and say with your hands spread open:)

Loving God, Creator of all that is,
here I am— today, in this place,
with all the senses you have given me.
Help me to use them to experience you more deeply.
You are present everywhere around me;
open me to know more of the many ways
that Your goodness surrounds me.
Thank you for this time to be with you and to listen to you.
Amen.

SAVORING:

Look at the leaf before you or one of the leaves on the branch, if it has any. Examine the intricate structure of the veins on the back of the leaf and of its edges and/or the structure to the branch. Notice its complexity and gracefulness. Are there any changes in color to various parts of the leaf or branch? Feel the texture; is it fuzzy or smooth? Does that change at all within the leaf or branch? Does it have much of a smell?

All Around Us

How would it feel to be part of this plant or shrub or tree, growing taller and stronger with each passing day, reaching toward the sun and the sky? Can you sense the life that was flowing through this living part of creation?

LISTENING (The Word of God):

Listen to one or more of these passages as you watch the candle play across the leaf or branch:

In the evening the dove came back to [Noah], and there in its bill was a plucked-off olive leaf So Noah knew that the waters [of the flood] had lessened on the earth. (Gen 8:11)

A shoot shall come out from the stump of Jesse, and a branch shall grow out of his roots. The spirit of the LORD shall rest on him, the spirit of wisdom and understanding, the spirit of counsel and might, the spirit of knowledge and the fear of the LORD. (Isa 11:1–2)

Abide in me as I abide in you. Just as the branch cannot bear fruit by itself unless it abides in the vine, neither can you unless you abide in me. I am the vine, you are the branches. Those who abide in me and I in them bear much fruit, because apart from me you can do nothing. (John 15:4–5)

CONSIDERING:

A leaf, and the branch that supports it, is a factory of life. Through photosynthesis it is able to use light energy to help turn one of our human waste products, carbon dioxide, into the oxygen and water we need to survive.

Life is always flowing through a branch and into its leaves, so much so that it's hard to say where one begins and the other ends. Each kind of plant has a unique kind of structure to its leaves and branches, and each individual leaf and branch will also look unique, just as each person does.

This life that we see in branches and leaves comes from roots deep beneath the soil, another set of "branches" below the ground that helps make possible the growth above ground.

In the Fall, when the leaves of all but the evergreens must separate from the branches in order to make room for new growth in the Spring,

A Leaf or Brach: Alive in Christ

the dying process within these branches and leaves results in a stunning display of colors, especially where nights are cold.

RESPONDING:

There are times when I also need to let go of certain parts of my life, certain places, and even certain people, in order to grow further or to let them grow.

God of all creation, help me to do that with the grace of my sisters and brothers, the leaves, knowing that you have some deeper life in store for me that I can't even begin to imagine. Are there some places in my life where I can look at letting go more than I have? Are there others around me that are struggling with letting go that I can help support or at least pray for?

Thank you for the wonder of trees and bushes, for all those who study and work with trees and plants. Whenever I see leaves or branches, help me to remember that it is only connected to you, "rooted" in you, that I can truly live, that you are the true source of all life and that "attached" to you I can flourish and become all that you dream for me. Amen.

CHAPTER 23

Ribbon or Bow: Gifts from God

Materials at hand: A ribbon or bow which could be used on a present, a candle as a prayer focus.

CENTERING (Light the candle and say with your hands spread open:)

Loving God, Creator of all that is,
here I am—today, in this place,
with all the senses you have given me.
Help me to use them to experience you more deeply.
You are present everywhere around me;
open me to know more of the many ways
that your goodness surrounds me.
Thank you for this time to be with you and to listen to you.
Amen.

SAVORING:

Consider the ribbon or bow before you and imagine the stories it—if it's used—or its "brothers and sisters" could tell about some of the gifts they've been on, the occasions for those presents, the time and energy in making or buying them, and the reception that greeted their opening. Recall the best present you ever received and why. What was it, and can you recall the details of the occasion when you received it?

Ribbon or Bow: Gifts from God

Try to predict what your fingers will experience as you touch what lies before you. How different is the somewhat sharp edge of the ribbon from the shinier, flat width of it? If you have a bow in front of you, trace its twists and turns with your eyes before using your fingers. Now touch the bow or ribbon with your fingers, noting whether it felt like you expected and what new information, if any, your fingers can give you.

Ribbons, and the wrapping paper they usually accompany, seem to be some of the least "useful" objects around us and yet they are more important than they seem; their only real purpose is to remind us to rejoice at the surprises and the gifts in our lives.

LISTENING:

Listen to one or more of these passages as you watch the candle play across the bow or ribbon:

In the time of King Herod, after Jesus was born in Bethlehem of Judea, wise men from the East came to Jerusalem, asking, "Where is the child who has been born king of the Jews? For we observed his star at its rising, and have come to pay him homage." . . . [T]hey set out; and there, ahead of them, went the star that they had seen at its rising, until it stopped over the place where the child was. When they saw that the star had stopped, they were overwhelmed with joy. On entering the house, they saw the child with Mary his mother; and they knelt down and paid him homage. Then, opening their treasure chests, they offered him gifts of gold, frankincense, and myrrh. (Matt 2:1–2,9–11)

What do you have that you did not receive? And if you received it, why do you boast as if it were not a gift? (1 Cor 4:7)

"Ask, and it will be given you; search, and you will find; knock, and the door will be opened for you. For everyone who asks receives, and everyone who searches finds, and for everyone who knocks, the door will be opened. Is there anyone among you who, if your child asks for bread, will give a stone? Or if the child asks for a fish, will give a snake? If you then, who are evil, know how to give good gifts to your children, how much more will your Father in heaven give good things to those who ask him! (Matt 7:7–11)

So when you are offering your gift at the altar, if you remember that your brother or sister has something against you, leave your gift there before the altar and go; first be reconciled to your brother or sister, and then come and offer your gift. (Matt 5:23–24)

... [A]bove all bless your Maker, who fills you with his good gifts. (Sir 32:13)

CONSIDERING:

Gifts are given for many different occasions; some celebrations may involve presents, but some may not. For example, birthdays, Christmas and Hanukkah usually involve gifts, but holidays of harvest or thanksgiving, such as our Thanksgiving Day, or of certain times of the year, such as New Year's or Mardi Gras, usually don't include gifts.

Holidays to mark remembrance of and respect for the dead, such as Memorial Day or El Dia de Los Muertos, may not involve gifts, just as days for commemorating an honored person or event, such as Lincoln's Birthday or the signing of the Declaration of Independence, also usually don't include presents. Holidays that celebrate a culture, such as the relatively recent Kwanzaa, may involve gifts or they may not. There are also certain situations where gifts may be expected, such as at a wedding and at traditional Native American potlatches.

In most situations, giving a gift is an attempt to say the "unsayable," to express through an object, and the thought that went into its choosing or making, what the one receiving the gift means to the gift giver.

For a person of faith, all of life is a gift, filled with many signs of God's goodness and love.

RESPONDING:

If all that we have received in our lives is gift, then, scripture reminds us, we must be generous in giving to others, especially those in need. The book of Sirach tells us:

Be generous when you worship the Lord, and do not stint the first fruits of your hands. With every gift show a cheerful face, and dedicate your tithe with gladness. Give to the Most High as he has given to you,

Ribbon or Bow: Gifts from God

and as generously as you can afford. For the Lord is the one who repays, and he will repay you sevenfold. (Sir 35:10–13)

Also in the little book of Tobit, the title character is giving words of wisdom to his son and reminds him:

[G]ive alms from your possessions, and do not let your eye begrudge the gift when you make it. Do not turn your face away from anyone who is poor, and the face of God will not be turned away from you. If you have many possessions, make your gift from them in proportion; if few, do not be afraid to give according to the little you have. (Tob 4:7–8)

What are some ways that I could be more generous to those around me in my life? Are there some things I have that I could share more readily, since they're really only on loan to me from God? What about some of the clothes or other possessions that I don't use any more? Can I share them with those who could really use them by giving them away? Let a friend know today what a gift he or she is to you.

God of all gifts in my life, thank you for the gift of life and for the many gifts I don't recognize, including that of my health. Bless those who make and sell gifts, those celebrating birthdays or other holidays today, and all those talented with many gifts from you.

Please help me to take another look at all the gifts you give me and even envision them with invisible bows and tags that say, "To you with great love, God." Your love is truly the greatest gift I could ever imagine. Amen.

CHAPTER 24

Feather or Egg: Consider the Birds of the Air

Materials at hand: A feather or egg (or bird's nest, if you have found one), with a candle as a prayer focus.

CENTERING (Light the candle and with your hands spread open:)

Loving God, Creator of all that is,
here I am—today, in this place,
with all the senses you have given me.
Help me to use them to experience you more deeply.
You are present everywhere around me;
open me to know more of the many ways
that your goodness surrounds me.
Thank you for this time to be with you and to listen to you.
Amen.

SAVORING:

Take a look at the feather or egg and take in as much information as you can with your eyes, so that you would be able to draw it, even if it were taken away. Look at it from many different directions to see it with new eyes. As your eyes take it in, predict what your fingers will feel as you touch it.

Then examine it with your fingers, noting the unique texture that helps it do what it needs to do: to protect—and to help fly, in the case of the feather. Does it help your sense of touch to close your eyes and

Feather or Egg: Consider the Birds of the Air

concentrate only on that information? Try to imagine how difficult it would be for a human engineer to design either of these important objects.

If you have a bird's nest, explore that with your senses also, being careful not to disturb this wonderful, nurturing place.

LISTENING:

Listen to one or more of these passages as you watch the candle play across the feather or egg (or nest) :

And God said, "Let the waters bring forth swarms of living creatures, and let birds fly above the earth across the dome of the sky." So God created ... every winged bird of every kind. And God saw that it was good. God blessed them, saying, "Be fruitful and multiply ... and let birds multiply on the earth." And there was evening and there was morning, the fifth day. (Gen 1:20–3)

How lovely is your dwelling place, O LORD of hosts! ... Even the sparrow finds a home, and the swallow a nest for herself, where she may lay her young, at your altars, O LORD of hosts, my King and my God. (Ps 84:1, 3)

When the Most High apportioned the nations, ... the Lord's own portion was his people, Jacob his allotted share. He sustained him in a desert land, in a howling wilderness waste; he shielded him, cared for him, guarded him as the apple of his eye. As an eagle stirs up its nest, and hovers over its young; as it spreads its wings, takes them up, and bears them aloft on its pinions, the LORD alone guided him ... (Deut 32:8–12)

Bless the Lord, all birds of the air; sing praise to him and highly exalt him forever. (Dan 3:80)

CONSIDERING:

Birds are fascinating creatures. They inhabit every continent and almost every island in the world and have adapted to many kinds of environments; they range in size from the ostrich, which may reach eight feet in height, to the bee hummingbird of Cuba, which measures 2.5 inches as an adult from the tip of its bill to the tip of its tail. Birds seem to have been

All Around Us

around a long time; the earliest fossils link birds to reptiles and probably to the dinosaurs.

In the Bible we find mention of many kinds of birds—from ravens to eagles to sparrows and swallows—and all four gospels record the important event of the Holy Spirit descending on Jesus in the form of a dove at the time of his baptism in the river Jordan by John the Baptist.

RESPONDING:

Three scripture passages which mention birds remind us how to live our lives—with kindness and honesty and without undue worry.

The book of Sirach reminds us of the importance of kindness, especially to our friends. "One who throws a stone at birds scares them away, and one who reviles a friend destroys a friendship." (Sir 22:20) The same book also describes the long-term importance of honesty. "Birds roost with their own kind, so honesty comes home to those who practice it." (Sir 27:9) Are there some ways that I can work on kindness—to friends or others—and on honesty in my life?

In the collection of sayings known as the Sermon on the Mount in Matthew's gospel, Jesus teaches us that watching birds—as he obviously has been—can help put life in better perspective:

Therefore I tell you, do not worry about your life, what you will eat or what you will drink, or about your body, what you will wear. Is not life more than food, and the body more than clothing? Look at the birds of the air; they neither sow nor reap nor gather into barns, and yet your heavenly Father feeds them. Are you not of more value than they? And can any of you by worrying add a single hour to your span of life? . . . But strive first for the kingdom of God and his righteousness, and all these things will be given to you as well. (Matt 6:25-7,33)

What have I been worrying about lately that I can let go of and turn over to you, loving God?

God of the skies and Creator of all that has feathers, thank you for the wonder of birds and their freedom and beauty. Bless all those who care for, work with and help protect the birds of our world.

Let birds help remind me of the need to be kind and honest and, most of all, not to worry about my life because you certainly care for me more tenderly than the most attentive mother bird hovering over her nest. Amen.

CHAPTER 25

Music: Make a Joyful Noise

Materials at hand: A music compact disc, cassette, or record—or a musical instrument or sheet music if you have either, with a candle as a prayer focus.

CENTERING (Light the candle and say with your hands spread open:)

Loving God, Creator of all that is,
here I am—today, in this place,
with all the senses you have given me.
Help me to use them to experience you more deeply.
You are present everywhere around me;
open me to know more of the many ways
that your goodness surrounds me.
Thank you for this time to be with you and to listen to you.
Amen.

SAVORING:

Before considering the role of music in your life, listen to what may seem like the absence of music: silence. Listen to the silence—or more likely at least a few sounds, in our noisy world—around you. Can you hear any birds chirping or the sound of any appliances or other motors running in your house or outside—or other noises? This silence and these sounds, even the beat of your heart, are all a part of the music of our lives, each sound with its own pitch and tempo.

Now look at the source(s) of music before you, whether recorded or live. For right now, disregard the specifics of the kind of music represented before you and think about music in general and its place in your life. Reflect on all the ways that music has been a part of your life, from lullabies and other songs when you were small through the singing of "Happy Birthday" each year as you grew to songs from school or camp in childhood, the music of your teen years and many other kinds of music that have filled your days in many ways to the present. Music gives us a way, both as individuals and as a community, to express what can't be said any other way. Music exists in every culture and is almost always a part of every celebration or ritual.

What is your favorite musical instrument and why? What about your favorite musician and/or piece of music? Think carefully about why it is your favorite; is there something important to your life that a particular song or musician helps express that can't be "said" any other way?

If you have a musical instrument before you, play a note or a chord and listen to it echo into the silence. (If you don't have a musical instrument, either play a very brief part of the recorded music before you or just hum a favorite melody.) Listen to it with your heart as well as with your ears.

How can vibrating sound waves make such an important difference in how we understand ourselves and feel about our lives? Perhaps they "resonate" in some way that we don't fully understand with the rhythms that are deep inside us. Whether recorded or live, music is indeed a rich part of our lives.

LISTENING:

Listen to one or more of these passages as you watch the candle play across the CD or tape, instrument or music:

It is good to give thanks to the LORD, to sing praises to your name, O Most High; to declare your steadfast love in the morning, and your faithfulness by night, to the music of the lute and the harp, to the melody of the lyre. For you, O LORD, have made me glad by your work; at the works of your hands I sing for joy. (Ps 92:1–4)

Music: Make a Joyful Noise

[The new king] David and all Israel were dancing before God with all their might, with song and lyres and harps and tambourines and cymbals and trumpets. (1 Chr 13:8)

Praise the LORD with the lyre; make melody to him with the harp of ten strings. Sing to him a new song; play skillfully on the strings, with loud shouts. For the word of the LORD is upright, and all his work is done in faithfulness. (Ps 33:2–4)

. . . be filled with the Spirit, as you sing psalms and hymns and spiritual songs among yourselves, singing and making melody to the Lord in your hearts, giving thanks to God the Father at all times and for everything in the name of our Lord Jesus Christ. (Eph 5:18–20)

Praise him with trumpet sound; praise him with lute and harp! Praise him with tambourine and dance; praise him with strings and pipe! Praise him with clanging cymbals; praise him with loud clashing cymbals! Let everything that breathes praise the LORD! Praise the LORD! (Ps 150:3–6)

CONSIDERING:

Music has been an important part of our human experience. Throughout history we have used it as we worked and played, and as we prayed, celebrated, danced, and even mourned. Music encompasses an incredible variety of sounds and tempos, from chants to electronic sounds, from opera to rap, from jazz to church bells, from reggae or klezmer to a quiet solo ballad. And the musical instruments used to make these sounds range from those we blow into (brass and woodwinds), those with strings that we pluck or bow (strings), those we hit in one way or another (percussion), and those with keyboards, as well as those that make their sounds through electronic means. The wonderful variety of our music is probably the closest we humans have to a universal language.

The recorded music we have today and its technology is easy for us to take for granted, but we should remember that it has existed for less than a century and a half. The process of recording music has gone from the mechanical processes of Thomas Edison's cylinders and then phonograph records to elecromagnetic tape recordings and the more recent digital forms—and who knows where in the future!

All Around Us

Before recordings, of course, the only way to listen to the music we can now hear at the flip of a switch would have been to hear the music performed in person—or to play it ourselves. Playing an instrument, while challenging, is a unique opportunity to express oneself. Whether we play an instrument ourselves or play recorded performances which past generations would have envied, music is an amazing gift in our lives.

RESPONDING:

Music suggests at least a couple of images for us to consider: that of harmony and of being God's "instrument."

If voices or instruments are "out of tune" with each other, we can often hear the dissonance. Sometimes in our lives we end up "out of tune" with those around us without realizing how it happened, and we need to work on ways to "harmonize" better with them. The writer of the book of Sirach reminds us, "The flute and the harp make sweet melody, but a pleasant voice is better than either." (Sir 40:21) Loving God, help me to "listen" with my heart for those places of harmony and to the other places where I need to work on "tuning up" the ways I speak to and deal with others so that I am more pleasant and respectful.

Have you ever thought of yourself as an instrument? After the account of Paul's dramatic conversion in the Acts of the Apostles, God speaks to a man named Ananias, telling him to seek Paul out and heal him of his temporary blindness. But Ananias objects because he has heard so much about how Paul has been persecuting the Christians. In answer God says to Ananias,"'Go, for he is an instrument whom I have chosen to bring my name before Gentiles and kings and before the people of Israel; I myself will show him how much he must suffer for the sake of my name.'" (Acts 9:15-6)

Although none of us is St. Paul, we all are "instruments" of God, chosen by God to "play" and "sing" certain "melodies" in our lives for God, songs that only we can make, by who we are and how we live. What kind of instrument do *you* see yourself to be in God's "hands?" What is *your* song?

Loving God of all music and harmony, please bless all those who play music, those who write it and those who teach others to play, and those who record and sell music and musical instruments. Help us to

Music: Make a Joyful Noise

understand each other better across many differences through the powerful language of music so that we might more fully sing your praises, God of all beauty and sound. Amen.

(You may want to try to chant the "Amen" or play your favorite music now.)

CHAPTER 26

Moon and Stars: Look Up and See

Materials at hand: Sit by a window on a moonlit and/or starry evening or go outside if the weather allows (or have a chart of the stars or a constellation in front of you), with a candle as a prayer focus.

CENTERING: (Light the candle and say with your hands spread open:)

Loving God, Creator of all that is,
here I am—today, in this place,
with all the senses You have given me.
Help me to use them to come to experience You more deeply
You are present everywhere around me;
open me to know more of the many ways
that Your goodness surrounds me.
Thank you for this time to be with You and to listen to You.
Amen.

SAVORING:

If you have a rather limited view of the moon or stars because of lights around you and cannot go where you can see them with less "light pollution," try to use your imagination about their clarity or recall a time when you were camping or in a less crowded area and able to see the moon and stars in all their glory. Take a careful and slow look around at what you

Moon and Stars: Look Up and See

see before you in the sky. (Or if you're not able to see the stars or moon and are looking at a star chart, remember what it's like to be outside under the night sky.)

If the moon is out, what phase is it in? Do you know how to tell if it's in its first quarter or last? Is it full or nearly so? If it were a new moon, you wouldn't see it at all. When do you first remember seeing the moon as a child and wondering about it? Imagine all the people throughout human history who have wondered about this presence in the night sky that changes throughout the month.

Look at the stars that are visible, not trying to identify constellations for now, even if you know how to recognize some. After looking carefully throughout the sky, then look again, this time looking for fainter stars that you couldn't see the first time but may be able to as your eyes get more used to the dark night sky. If it's a really clear night and you're away from bright lights, the number of stars that are visible is staggering, and the vastness of the night sky and the universe can begin to overwhelm us.

Now pick out one of those stars—or constellations, if you have a favorite and can recognize it—and try to imagine how long the light you're seeing from that star (or stars) has been traveling to get to your eyes. Chances are that the light left the star before you were born—or at least a good many years ago. (The closest star to our solar system is more than four light-years away; that means that the light we see now left there over four years ago.) Could there be intelligent life there also staring into space, wondering about what they can see? We have no evidence of life elsewhere so far, but scientists still really don't know for sure.

Do you have any favorite memories of sleeping under the stars when camping or even in your backyard? Many ancient civilizations worshiped the moon and stars, but the Jewish people saw them as being created by the one God. Looking up at the incredible complexity before us in the night sky, it's so easy to exclaim with the psalmist, "When I look at your heavens, the work of your fingers, the moon and the stars that you have established; what are human beings that you are mindful of them, mortals that you care for them?" [Ps 8:3–4]

LISTENING:

Listen to one or more of these passages as you watch the candle and look at the moon and stars (or at the chart):

All Around Us

And God said, "Let there be lights in the dome of the sky to separate the day from the night; and let them be for signs and for seasons and for days and years, and let them be lights in the dome of the sky to give light upon the earth." And it was so. God made the two great lights—the greater light to rule the day and the lesser light to rule the night—and the stars. God set them in the dome of the sky to give light upon the earth, to rule over the day and over the night, and to separate the light from the darkness. And God saw that it was good. And there was evening and there was morning, the fourth day. (Gen 1:14–19)

Praise him, sun and moon; praise him, all you shining stars! (Ps 148:3)

It is the moon that marks the changing seasons, governing the times, their everlasting sign. From the moon comes the sign for festal days, a light that wanes when it completes its course. The new moon, as its name suggests, renews itself; how marvelous it is in this change, a beacon to the hosts on high, shining in the vault of the heavens! The glory of the stars is the beauty of heaven, a glittering array in the heights of the Lord. On the orders of the Holy One they stand in their appointed places; they never relax in their watches. (Sir 43:6–10)

[God] brought [Abram] outside and said, "Look toward heaven and count the stars, if you are able to count them." Then he said to him, "So shall your descendants be." (Gen 15:5)

Bless the Lord, sun and moon; sing praise to him and highly exalt him forever. Bless the Lord, stars of heaven; sing praise to him and highly exalt him forever. (Dan 3:62–63)

[The wise men from the East] set out; and there, ahead of them, went the star that they had seen at its rising, until it stopped over the place where the child was. When they saw that the star had stopped, they were overwhelmed with joy. On entering the house, they saw the child with Mary his mother; and they knelt down and paid him homage. (Matt 2:9–11)

CONSIDERING:

The moon and stars have been objects of fascination for humans as long as we have been on this planet.

Moon and Stars: Look Up and See

Our moon is a kind of natural satellite, one quarter the width of planet Earth, with a volume fifty times less than ours. It is about as old as this planet: over four and a half billion years. It orbits us every twenty nine and a half days, but we only see one side of it because the other side is always facing away from us. Even after six manned landings—and many other unmanned ones—we still are learning more about the surface and chemical make-up of the moon. We do know that the moon's gravitational pull on the earth is largely responsible for the ocean tides around our world.

It is estimated that there are about 8,000 stars visible from the earth with the naked eye, half of those from the Northern Hemisphere and half from the South. And only half again of those are visible at any given time. Since the ancient Greeks or earlier, there has been an awareness of an order in the universe, of certain patterns of stars that we call constellations that seem to travel in the sky seasonally. (Actually, it's the earth that changes in its angle of rotation, and that causes the "shifts" in where we find certain stars and constellations. The stars and constellations are also traveling, but the distances involved are so great that those changes are apparent only after centuries.) Have you ever been to a planetarium to see a demonstration of the arrangement of the stars and how the seasons affect what we see and where we see it?

Within our Milky Way galaxy there are hundreds of billions of stars, and there are, in turn, several hundred million other galaxies visible through larger modern telescopes. These numbers rapidly become unimaginable to us. The stars that we can see are closest to our solar system in our galaxy. Their known size can vary from 400 times the size of our sun to 100 times smaller than our sun, although there may well be stars both smaller and larger than that.

When we think about the moon—and even more the stars—our awareness of, and awe at, God's endless creativity and goodness really starts to "take off."

RESPONDING:

Looking at the night sky gives us a renewed sense of the vastness of God and God's love for us. Psalm 147 expresses it this way: "[The Lord] determines the number of the stars; he gives to all of them their names. Great is

our Lord, and abundant in power; his understanding is beyond measure."
(Ps 147:4–5)

Besides a sense of awe at the universe, there are also many questions that our space exploration raises: How did the stars and planets come to exist in the way they do today? How can we more fully understand some of what we seem to observe through our telescopes, such as quasars and black holes? These are questions that keep scientists busy trying to understand the data that they continue to discover.

But perhaps one of the greatest gifts we have received from our exploration of space is the picture of Earth taken from space, the single powerful image of this fragile planet that we all share and of which we need to take special care.

Loving God of all the universe, both known and unknown, help us all to look with new eyes at the gift of life all around us on our planet. Help us to reverence the richness and diversity of plants and animals, seasons and other people on this our blue-and-green home.

Help me to be more aware of ways that I can help care for the earth, from recycling to alternate forms of transportation. Bless all those who work to help improve the environment and save it from over-consumption.

Bless also those involved in the study and exploration of space, and thank You for all they have helped us learn about the incredibly vast and complex universe You have made.

Help me to remember Your goodness in a special way whenever I see the moon and stars. Amen.

CHAPTER 27

Window: Let Me See Your Love

Materials at hand: Sit by a window so that you can focus more on the window itself than on what you can see through the window, and have a candle as a prayer focus.

CENTERING (Light the candle and say with your hands spread open:)

Loving God, Creator of all that is,
here I am—today, in this place,
with all the senses you have given me.
Help me to use them to experience you more deeply.
You are present everywhere around me;
open me to know more of the many ways
that your goodness surrounds me.
Thank you for this time to be with you and to listen to you.
Amen.

SAVORING:

Look at the window before you, which is basically a hole in the wall covered instead with glass. Imagine that the glass was gone and that it was an opening, as it was when it was being built. Also try to imagine a completely different scene outside the window than what you can see when you look out. What would you change it to? Why?

Take a close look at the window itself and then close your eyes and try to picture and describe the details of it. Does it open? How? Does it have a screen or a storm window on it? What kind of frame does it have? Is there a curtain or drape or blind or shade of some kind that can cover it at night or when you want to shut out the light or have privacy? So often we tend to ignore the windows in our lives because we're so busy looking through them to what's beyond.

Touch the window, or at least its frame, after predicting what your fingers will find. Is the glass cold or warm? Is it smoother than you would have expected? Try to imagine all that this window has "seen:" many seasons that have come and gone and much life, both inside and outside of it.

Try to imagine what someone looking in through your window would see. Is there much difference between outside and inside? Think of all the windows you have looked out of, as well as into, in your life; try to list as many kinds as you can—car, plane, train, bus, subway, windows in public buildings, stores, church, and so on.

Windows are part of our lives every day; they help make our days brighter, safer and more interesting.

LISTENING:

Listen to one or more of these passages as you watch the candle play across the window:

In the six hundredth year of Noah's life, in the second month, on the seventeenth day of the month, on that day all the fountains of the great deep burst forth, and the windows of the heavens were opened. The rain fell on the earth forty days and forty nights. On the very same day Noah with . . . [his family] entered the ark, they and every wild animal of every kind, and all domestic animals of every kind, and every creeping thing that creeps on the earth, and every bird of every kind—every bird, every winged creature. They went into the ark with Noah, two and two of all flesh in which there was the breath of life . . .

At the end of forty days Noah opened the window of the ark that he had made and sent out the raven; and it went to and fro until the waters were dried up from the earth. Then he sent out the dove from him, to see if the waters had subsided from the face of the ground; but the dove found no place to set its foot, and it returned to him to the ark, for the waters

Window: Let Me See Your Love

were still on the face of the whole earth. So he put out his hand and took it and brought it into the ark with him. He waited another seven days, and again he sent out the dove from the ark; and the dove came back to him in the evening, and there in its beak was a freshly plucked olive leaf; so Noah knew that the waters had subsided from the earth. (Gen 7:11–15,8:6–11)

O my strength, I will watch for you; for you, O God, are my fortress. (Ps 59:9)

See, I have refined you, but not like silver; I have tested you in the furnace of adversity. (Is 48:10)

On that day Sarah was grieved in spirit and wept . . . At that same time, with hands outstretched toward the window, she prayed and said, "Blessed are you, merciful God! Blessed is your name forever; let all your works praise you forever. And now, Lord, I turn my face to you, and raise my eyes toward you . . . hear me in my disgrace." (Tob 3:10–12, 15)

CONSIDERING:

It's hard to imagine our world without windows or without the glass that fills them. The ordinary house in ancient Biblical times probably had no more than one window, which would help cool the house in summer, but in the winter it may have been filled with stones in order to try to keep the cold out, in addition to the mats or shutters that would usually cover it at night.

Glass was used in windows from the first century AD, and originally came from cylinders that were blown and then cut and flattened into sheets. In order to try to overcome the variations in thickness from this and other methods, the first plate glass was made in France in 1668. However the glass is formed, an important part of making glass is annealing, a process that heats and then slowly cools it so that it is less brittle and prone to breakage. The basic ingredient is silica, usually from sand; we use glass all around us every day without a second thought for the amazing way that sand becomes something we can see through with little or no distortion.

Whether it's stained glass, etched or leaded glass or just plain panes, windows are "clearly" important in our lives.

RESPONDING:

There are many things in our lives that can become "windows" of a sort for us, including books, movies, television, travel, other people, even our computers—many of which come complete with an operating system called Windows.

What, or who, has been most helpful for you as a "window?" How has it/this person brought light or clarity or a new point of view into your life? Try to be specific. Is there anyone that you have been, or could be, a "window" for? How? One of the ways that we can be thankful for the mentors and teachers—or windows—in our lives is to help others in turn.

Loving God of skylights and shutters, of light and darkness, help us to appreciate the windows in our lives, both those "eyes" of the buildings we inhabit and the people, places and things that help us look again at our world and our lives.

Bless all those who make, install and clean windows. Bless, too, those who teach in all kinds of ways, helping their students to open up "windows" to the world. Help us to be "open" to the many ways you show yourself to us, just outside our windows. Amen.

CHAPTER 28

Basket: Woven In Love

Materials at hand: A candle as a prayer focus and one or more baskets.

CENTERING (Light the candle and say with your hands spread open:)

Loving God, Creator of all that is,
here I am—today, in this place,
with all the senses you have given me.
Help me to use them to experience you more deeply.
You are present everywhere around me;
open me to know more of the many ways
that your goodness surrounds me.
Thank you for this time to be with you and to listen to you.
Amen.

SAVORING:

Notice the basket (or baskets) before you—the overall shape and texture, the height and width and even the thickness of each. Try to follow with your eyes some of the strands of the weaving on the side of the basket(s) facing you. Imagine how the fibers will feel as you touch them but also imagine how they must have felt to the person who was weaving them together when they were wet and more pliable. Notice how the light plays across the basket and all the variations of color within the one basket because of the differences of depth on the surface of the basket. Imagine, too, the journey this basket has had, from the person who made it to where it would be sold and then consider all the uses and all the objects that this basket has—or could have—held since then. (If you have more than one basket before you, do this for each basket and notice the similarities and differences between them.)

Now touch the basket (or baskets) with your eyes closed to help you concentrate on tactile information. How does what your fingers are telling you compare with what your eyes predicted? With your fingers try to follow one strand of the basket from the center where it begins out to the rim of the basket, marveling as you do at all the twists and turns it takes along the way.

Is there a smell to the basket? Our sense of smell often carries a deep connection to our memories. Can you imagine the fibers of this basket when they were growing and alive, before they ever became a basket? Listen for any sound the basket(s) make(s) when you touch and handle it.

Baskets are important inventions and also multisensory experiences.

LISTENING:

Listen to one or more of these passages as you watch the candle play across the basket or baskets:

Now a man from the house of Levi went and married a Levite woman. The woman conceived and bore a son; and when she saw that he was a fine baby, she hid him three months. When she could hide him no longer she got a papyrus basket for him, and plastered it with bitumen and pitch; she put the child in it and placed it among the reeds on the bank of the river.

His sister stood at a distance, to see what would happen to him. The daughter of Pharaoh came down to bathe at the river, while her attendants walked beside the river. She saw the basket among the reeds and sent her maid to bring it. When she opened it, she saw the child. He was crying, and she took pity on him. "This must be one of the Hebrews' children," she said. Then his sister said to Pharaoh's daughter, "Shall I go and get you a nurse from the Hebrew women to nurse the child for you?" Pharaoh's daughter said to her, "Yes." So the girl went and called the child's mother.

Pharaoh's daughter said to her, "Take this child and nurse it for me, and I will give you your wages." So the woman took the child and nursed it. When the child grew up, she brought him to Pharaoh's daughter, and she took him as her son. She named him Moses, "because," she said, "I drew him out of the water." (Exod 2:1–10)

When you have come into the land that the LORD your God is giving you as an inheritance to possess, and you possess it, and settle in it, you shall take some of the first of all the fruit of the ground, which you harvest from the land that the LORD your God is giving you, and you shall put it in a basket and go to the place that the LORD your God will choose as a dwelling for his name. You shall go to the priest who is in office at that time, and say to him, "Today I declare to the LORD your God that I have come into the land that the LORD swore to our ancestors to give us." When the priest takes the basket from your hand and sets it down before the altar of the LORD your God, you shall make this response before the LORD your God: "A wandering Aramean was my ancestor; he went down into Egypt and lived there as an alien, few in number, and there he became a great nation, mighty and populous. When the Egyptians treated us harshly and afflicted us, by imposing hard labor on us, we cried to the LORD, the God of our ancestors; the LORD heard our voice and saw our affliction, our toil, and our oppression. The LORD brought us out of Egypt with a mighty hand and an outstretched arm, with a terrifying display of power, and with signs and wonders; and he brought us into this place and gave us this land, a land flowing with milk and honey. So now I bring the first of the fruit of the ground that you, O LORD, have given me." You shall set it down before the LORD your God and bow down before the LORD your God. (Deut 26:1–10)

And immediately something like scales fell from [Saul's] eyes, and his sight was restored. Then he got up and was baptized, and after taking some food, he regained his strength. For several days he was with the disciples in Damascus, and immediately he began to proclaim Jesus in the synagogues, saying, "He is the Son of God." All who heard him were amazed and said, "Is not this the man who made havoc in Jerusalem among those who invoked this name? And has he not come here for the purpose of bringing them bound before the chief priests?" Saul became increasingly more powerful and confounded the Jews who lived in Damascus by proving that Jesus was the Messiah. After some time had

All Around Us

passed, the Jews plotted to kill him, but their plot became known to Saul. They were watching the gates day and night so that they might kill him; but his disciples took him by night and let him down through an opening in the wall, lowering him in a basket. (Acts 9:18–25)

CONSIDERING:

Basket making is one of the oldest human handicrafts. Since prehistoric times people have made baskets out of the materials at hand—often grasses, leaves, stalks and other plant materials—to use as containers.

Baskets can be made from soft or hard materials, but the latter have to be dried and then soaked to make them flexible and workable. There are four basic methods of basket making—weaving, twining, plaiting and coiling—which involve a variety of ways that the warp, or spokes, of the basket interconnect with the weft, or weavers, which go in and out of the spokes. Relatively few tools are needed to weave baskets, and many intricate styles have been produced by so-called primitive peoples, becoming a true art form.

Baskets have been used for many purposes through the centuries, including holding the fruits of the harvest, and so have often become associated with thanksgiving for God's gracious love and generous bounty. For both the infant Moses and the adult Saul just after his conversion experience, baskets were a means of deliverance and safety—not only for their own sake but so that they could lead their people closer to God.

Today baskets are usually imported from other parts of the world, and they continue to perform decorative as well as practical functions.

RESPONDING:

Loving God, who weaves our lives together with your love, like the most intricate of baskets, thank you for all those who make and sell baskets and who have through all the ages, both for their living and as a hobby. I pray today for all those who serve food in baskets, who bake or grow or pick the food that is found there. Bless those places, like churches, where baskets are a means of collecting money to be shared with others in need. I even pray for those who may fly in baskets under hot air balloons.

Jesus uses the image of a basket to remind us of our call to share our gifts and our faith with others: "You are the light of the world. A city built on a hill cannot be hid. No one after lighting a lamp puts it under the bushel basket, but on the lampstand, and it gives light to all in the house. In the same way, let your light shine before others, so that they may see your good works and give glory to your Father in heaven." (Matt 5:14–16) Loving God, help me to not be afraid to share the gifts you have given me with others and also to encourage others to share their gifts.

And the book of Deuteronomy reminds us, too, of the blessings that are ours when we are open to God's love and promises in our lives: "If you will only obey the LORD your God, by diligently observing all his commandments that I am commanding you today, the LORD your God will set you high above all the nations of the earth; all these blessings shall come upon you and overtake you, if you obey the LORD your God: . . . Blessed shall be your basket and your kneading bowl. Blessed shall you be when you come in, and blessed shall you be when you go out." (Deut 28:1–2, 5–6)

Basket weaver God, thank you for the beauty of the "basket" of my life and for all the blessings and experiences you have woven into it; help me to continue to be grateful for all that fills my basket. Amen.

CHAPTER 29

Seashell: Like the Sands of the Sea

Materials at hand: A seashell or two, a small piece of driftwood or a picture of the ocean or sea shore or a lake, with a candle as a prayer focus.

CENTERING (Light the candle and say with your hands spread open:)

Loving God, Creator of all that is,
here I am—today, in this place,
with all the senses you have given me.
Help me to use them to experience you more deeply.
You are present everywhere around me;
open me to know more of the many ways
that your goodness surrounds me.
Thank you for this time to be with you and to listen to you.
Amen.

SAVORING:

Look at the shell(s) or the driftwood or picture before you. Picture them and yourself on a beach and fill in the rest of the "information:" the sounds, smells and other sights around you at the seashore. Listen for birds and for the sound of the waves as they crash powerfully away from the shore and as they gently lap the shore. Smell the salt water and the seaweed or whatever you are used to by the water. Is the beach you stand

Seashell: Like the Sands of the Sea

on sandy or rocky? Is there a breeze? Are you alone or are there other people enjoying being at the beach, too? Hold the shell(s) and consider its former resident(s) or handle the driftwood and reflect on the beating from tides that it must have undergone.

Recall some of your favorite memories at the beach. Were you swimming, fishing, sunbathing, digging for clams or just looking for shells or other "treasures?" What is it that you like best about spending time there? Whether ocean or lake, river or sea, there are so many signs of life on the water's shore that help remind us that water and land are not so different from each other after all.

LISTENING:

Listen to one or more of these passages as you watch the candle play across the seashell or driftwood or picture:

And God said, "Let the waters bring forth swarms of living creatures . . . So God created the great sea monsters and every living creature that moves, of every kind, with which the waters swarm, and every winged bird of every kind. And God saw that it was good. God blessed them, saying, "Be fruitful and multiply and fill the waters in the seas, and let birds multiply on the earth." And there was evening and there was morning, the fifth day. (Gen 1:20–23)

Then Moses stretched out his hand over the sea. The LORD drove the sea back by a strong east wind all night, and turned the sea into dry land; and the waters were divided. The Israelites went into the sea on dry ground, the waters forming a wall for them on their right and on their left. The Egyptians pursued, and went into the sea after them, all of Pharaoh's horses, chariots, and chariot drivers . . . Then the LORD said to Moses, "Stretch out your hand over the sea, so that the water may come back upon the Egyptians, upon their chariots and chariot drivers." So Moses stretched out his hand over the sea, and at dawn the sea returned to its normal depth . . . The waters returned and covered the chariots and the chariot drivers, the entire army of Pharaoh that had followed them into the sea; not one of them remained. But the Israelites walked on dry ground through the sea, the waters forming a wall for them on their right and on their left. (Exod 14:21–3, 26–29)

More majestic than the thunders of mighty waters, more majestic than the waves of the sea, majestic on high is the LORD! (Ps 93:4)

The angel of the LORD called to Abraham a second time from heaven, and said, " . . . I will indeed bless you, and I will make your offspring as numerous as the stars of heaven and as the sand that is on the seashore. And . . . by your offspring shall all the nations of the earth gain blessing for themselves, because you have obeyed my voice." (Gen 22:15,17–18)

The sand of the sea, the drops of rain, and the days of eternity—who can count them? (Sir 1:2)

Bless the Lord, seas and rivers; sing praise to him and highly exalt him forever. Bless the Lord, you whales and all that swim in the waters; sing praise to him and highly exalt him forever. (Dan 3:78–79)

Just after daybreak, Jesus stood on the beach; but the disciples did not know that it was Jesus . . . When they had gone ashore, they saw a charcoal fire there, with fish on it, and bread. Jesus said to them, "Bring some of the fish that you have just caught." . . . [He] said to them, "Come and have breakfast." Now none of the disciples dared to ask him, "Who are you?" because they knew it was the Lord. Jesus came and took the bread and gave it to them, and did the same with the fish. (John 21:4,9–10,12–13)

CONSIDERING:

Scientists tell us that over seventy percent of the earth's surface is covered by oceans and seas. In a sense, the world is an ocean, interrupted here or there by the islands that we call continents.

Ocean beaches are places of constant change, busier than they may appear. Whether the shore is rocky, muddy, or sandy and whether it's high tide or low will make a difference as to what life forms are evident, but much is happening below the surface—literally—and many of the creatures involved, such as plankton, are not visible to the human eye without a microscope's help. On the other hand, the ocean is also home to the largest animals that have ever lived, larger even than the dinosaurs that once roamed the earth.

Oceans, seas and rivers are important as sources of transportation, as well as for recreation and seafood. While some people may live by water, many of us only end up spending time by a lake, river or ocean on vacation, if at all.

Although the area where Jesus lived was close to the Mediterranean Sea, he was more familiar with the Sea of Galilee, which is more technically a lake, sometimes called Lake Tiberias. It is below sea level, cool and clear, and at the time it was the center of an extensive fishing industry and a rich source of fish and where many of Jesus' disciples fished for a living until they followed Jesus. It was also where Capernaum, a town where much of his public life took place, was located. Jesus seemed to like to spend time around the water, as most of us do.

Whether as an ocean, bay, lake or river, water continues to give life both to the land and to each of us.

RESPONDING:

The image of the waves breaking on the shore and the shell(s) before us can help us consider our relationship to God in several ways.

We know that the waves continue to lap against the shore, day and night, no matter what the weather. In the same way God continues to "bathe" us with care and love, even when we're not aware of it, giving life to us just as the tides bring moisture, nourishment and minerals to the shore.

And just as God helps the mollusks—animals like clams or oysters or snails who make their own shells—provide a home for themselves, God will also provide for each of us, often by giving us the ways to help ourselves, if we only take advantage of the opportunities before us.

However, the epistle of James reminds us that it may not be easy to remember God's love at times: "If any of you is lacking in wisdom, ask God, who gives to all generously and ungrudgingly, and it will be given you. But ask in faith, never doubting, for the one who doubts is like a wave of the sea, driven and tossed by the wind; for the doubter, being double-minded and unstable in every way, must not expect to receive anything from the Lord." (Jas 1:5–7)

Loving God, creator of the oceans and the shores, of lakes and rivers, and of everything that dwells on and in them, help me to see the complexity of all that you have created as a reminder of the many ways that you provide for each one of us. Thank you for all of life, from the largest whale to the smallest bit of plankton. Thank you for all who work to help preserve endangered plants and animals in or near the waters of our earth.

Bless those who live or work on the water, those who fish for sport or for a living and those who use boats or ships for recreation, travel or work; keep them safe. Please help us learn how to protect the waters of our earth from further pollution and how to clean up the problems we have already created.

Thank you for the amazing interaction between water and shore in the world in which we live. And help me to remember your faithful, tender love for me whenever I see a shell or a piece of driftwood. Amen.

CHAPTER 30

Name: I Have Called You

Materials at hand: A piece of paper on which you have lettered your full name in the center—including confirmation name and maiden name, if those apply—and around it your signature and any forms of your name or nicknames you have had, as well as your initials, also a' candle as a prayer focus. (You could use a plaque or certificate that has your name on it instead, if you'd rather.)

CENTERING: (Light the candle and say with your hands spread open:)

Loving God, Creator of all that is,
here I am—today, in this place,
with all the senses you have given me.
Help me to use them to experience you more deeply.
You are present everywhere around me;
open me to know more of the many ways
that your goodness surrounds me.
Thank you for this time to be with you and to listen to you.
Amen.

SAVORING (Senses at Work):

Take a look at the name before you. Trace it with your finger or doodle around it if you'd like. Do you know what your name means and the story behind your being given that name? If you have any nicknames, remind yourself of what their history is.

Say your name aloud softly so that your voice and your ears also get involved. Are there parts of your name you like better than others? Have you ever met anyone who had exactly the same name? What would be your ideal name if you could have picked your own? Listen in your head to people you know and love saying your name, not just in the present but throughout your life. How does that feel?

In one sense, a name is just some sounds or some marks on paper or another surface, but because of who each of us is and our own unique history, a name is so much more than that.

LISTENING:

Listen to one or more of these passages as you watch the candle play across the paper with your name on it:

So out of the ground the LORD God formed every animal of the field and every bird of the air, and brought them to the man to see what he would call them; and whatever the man called every living creature, that was its name. (Gen 2:19)

But now thus says the LORD, he who created you, O Jacob, he who formed you, O Israel: Do not fear, for I have redeemed you; I have called you by name, you are mine. When you pass through the waters, I will be with you; and through the rivers, they shall not overwhelm you; when you walk through fire you shall not be burned, and the flame shall not consume you. For I am the LORD your God, the Holy One of Israel, your Savior. (Isa 43:1–3)

Bless the LORD, O my soul, and all that is within me, bless his holy name. (Ps 103:1)

Early on the first day of the week, while it was still dark, Mary Magdalene came to the tomb and saw that the stone had been removed from the tomb . . . Mary stood weeping outside the tomb. As she wept, she bent over to look into the tomb; and she saw two angels in white, sitting where the body of Jesus had been lying, one at the head and the other at the feet. They said to her, "Woman, why are you weeping?" She said to them, "They have taken away my Lord, and I do not know where they have laid him." When she had said this, she turned around and saw Jesus standing there, but she did not know that it was Jesus. Jesus said to her, "Woman, why are you weeping? Whom are you looking for?" Supposing him to be the gardener, she said to him, "Sir, if you have carried him away, tell me where you have laid him, and I will take him away." Jesus said to her, "Mary!" She turned and said to him in Hebrew, "Rabbouni!" (which means Teacher). (John 20:1,11–16)

"For where two or three are gathered in my name, I am there among them." (Matt 18:20)

But Moses said to God, "Who am I that I should go to Pharaoh, and bring the Israelites out of Egypt? . . . If I come to the Israelites and say to them, 'The God of your ancestors has sent me to you,' and they ask me, 'What is his name?' what shall I say to them?" God said to Moses, "I AM WHO I AM." He said further, "Thus you shall say to the Israelites, 'I AM has sent me to you.'" God also said to Moses, "Thus you shall say to the Israelites, 'The LORD, the God of your ancestors, the God of Abraham, the God of Isaac, and the God of Jacob, has sent me to you': This is my name forever, and this my title for all generations. (Exod 3:11, 13–15)

All the nations you have made shall come and bow down before you, O Lord, and shall glorify your name. For you are great and do wondrous things; you alone are God. Teach me your way, O LORD, that I may walk in your truth; give me an undivided heart to revere your name. I give thanks to you, O Lord my God, with my whole heart, and I will glorify your name forever. (Ps 86:9–12)

From the rising of the sun to its setting the name of the LORD is to be praised. (Ps 113:3)

CONSIDERING:

Names *are* important. The study of names and their origins is called onomastics, after "onoma," the Greek word for name. First names, also called forenames or Christian names, existed much earlier than family names. But things finally became too confusing if there were two people of the same name in the same area, and surnames gradually came into usage.

All Around Us

There are many origins for the surnames we use today, from places nearby (Woods, Hill, Church) to certain trades (Smith, Miller, Cooper, Baker) to one's parentage, with, for example, "Mac-" or "Mc-" in Ireland or Scotland, "-son" in England and "-sen" in Scandinavia, and "-ben-" in Hebrew meaning "the child of." More women than in the past have decided to retain their surnames after marriage rather than taking their husbands' surname, sometimes hyphenating their last names or having a different last name from that of their husbands.

Many cultures have a different order for names than what we may be used to; in some countries the family name comes first and then the personal name. The Native American and Asian naming traditions are unique and especially interesting.

In the ancient Hebrew culture, as well as many others, one's name was part of one's character and identity and told something about that person; it was more than just an arbitrary choice. When there was a major change in a person's life, that would often be shown in a change in the person's name, as when Abram and Sarai became Abraham and Sarah and when Jacob became Israel.

The one choosing the name in such cultures had a certain amount of power and control over the one being named, as the human did in naming the animals in the second chapter of Genesis. But God's name was so holy and beyond human control or power that at times in Judaism it hasn't even been said. The role of the prophets, who were sent to speak in God's name, often was to remind the people of Israel not to forget God's name and God's holiness in their lives.

RESPONDING:

A renewed awareness of the importance of God's name, and my own, reminds me to make good choices, to always remember God's presence in my life and to ask for whatever I need.

My name, in the sense of my reputation, is precious, as the book of Sirach reminds us; therefore, I always need to act in such a way that I will be proud of what I did later. "Have regard for your name, since it will outlive you longer than a thousand hoards of gold. The days of a good life are numbered, but a good name lasts forever." (Sir 41:12–13)

For St. Paul *the* name in his life was that of Jesus, and he reminds the Christians in Colossus that everything they do should be done in Christ:

"... whatever you do, in word or deed, do everything in the name of the Lord Jesus, giving thanks to God the Father through him." (Col 3:17)

Jesus encouraged his disciples—and us—to ask for anything we need in prayer in His name: "Very truly, I tell you, if you ask anything of the Father in my name, he will give it to you. Until now you have not asked for anything in my name. Ask and you will receive, so that your joy may be complete." (John 16:23-24)

God of all names and Name above all others, please help those who don't know how special they—and their names—are and also those who may be unsure of their backgrounds because of adoption or other problems in their lives. Please bless all those who work with many names every day in offices, schools, and other institutions throughout the world.

Thank you for my name and for who I am, and help me to appreciate your many gifts to me again whenever I hear my name. Amen.

(You may find it to be a helpful prayer exercise sometime to try to write down the names of all the people who have been a part of your life. Although some of those relationships may have been difficult, it is usually rather overwhelming to see all the gifts that have been a part of your history and your "name.")

CHAPTER 31

Favorite Smell: A Pleasing Fragrance

Materials at hand: A favorite smell of yours (perhaps a scented candle, incense, or oil or perfume or even a favorite food or a picture of the source of a favorite smell) with a cover over it, and a candle as a prayer focus.

CENTERING (Light the candle and say with your hands spread open:)

Loving God, Creator of all that is,
here I am—today, in this place,
with all the senses you have given me.
Help me to use them to experience you more deeply.
You are present everywhere around me;
open me to know more of the many ways
that your goodness surrounds me.
Thank you for this time to be with you and to listen to you.
Amen.

SAVORING:

Before uncovering the source of the smell that you have before you, try to imagine what the smell will be like. Are there any words that come to mind to try to describe the smell? (Smell is such a strong sense but also one that is difficult to describe.)

Favorite Smell: A Pleasing Fragrance

Now uncover the source of the smell and wait for the aroma to reach your nose. Did it take very long? Did it build in strength or was it strong from the beginning? If the smell spread as fast as it did toward your nose, try to envision the way the fragrance has spread in all directions from its source, among the molecules of air around it. Did the smell match what you predicted and were expecting? Are there any other words that come to mind now about the actual experience of the smell? Why are smells so hard to describe, do you think?

Like hearing, smell is one of the senses that we can't "shut off" like we can shut our eyes and block out our sight; our noses will usually pick up what is around us whether we want them to or not, although some noses seem to be much more sensitive than others.

What are some of your other favorite smells besides the one before you? Are they included in this list? (*Try to recall as much as you can the smell of each one before reading the next in the list:*) Roast turkey, fresh-brewed coffee, after a rain or thunderstorm, popcorn, an evergreen tree, a baby after a bath, cinnamon rolls, an ocean beach, barbequed meat with sauce, garlic, a rose (or lilac or hyacinth), chocolate, freshly-mown grass, wood smoke, newly-tilled soil in a garden, chocolate chip cookies, apple pie, the soap or shampoo smell from a bath or shower. (What other favorite smells would you add to this list?)

Loving God, thank you for the wonder-full gift of the sense of smell.

LISTENING:

Listen to one or more of these passages as you watch the candle play across the source of the fragrance:

Send out fragrance like incense, and put forth blossoms like a lily. Scatter the fragrance, and sing a hymn of praise; bless the Lord for all his works. (Sir 39:14)

The LORD said to Moses: Take sweet spices, stacte, and onycha, and galbanum, sweet spices with pure frankincense (an equal part of each), and make an incense blended as by the perfumer, seasoned with salt, pure and holy; and you shall beat some of it into powder, and put part of it before the covenant in the tent of meeting where I shall meet with you; it shall be for you most holy. When you make incense according to this composition, you shall not make it for yourselves; it shall be regarded by you as holy to the LORD. Whoever makes any like it to use as perfume shall be cut off from the people. (Exod 30:34–38)

I call upon you, O LORD; come quickly to me; give ear to my voice when I call to you. Let my prayer be counted as incense before you, and the lifting up of my hands as an evening sacrifice. (Ps 141:1–2)

Six days before the Passover Jesus came to Bethany, the home of Lazarus, whom he had raised from the dead. There they gave a dinner for him. Martha served, and Lazarus was one of those at the table with him. Mary took a pound of costly perfume made of pure nard, anointed Jesus' feet, and wiped them with her hair. The house was filled with the fragrance of the perfume. (John 12:1–3)

And I saw the seven angels who stand before God, and seven trumpets were given to them. Another angel with a golden censer came and stood at the altar; he was given a great quantity of incense to offer with the prayers of all the saints on the golden altar that is before the throne. And the smoke of the incense, with the prayers of the saints, rose before God from the hand of the angel. (Rev 8:2–4)

CONSIDERING:

We are able to smell largely because of the olfactory nerves within our noses, and those same nerves are responsible for much of our sense of taste, which is often highly dependent on our sense of smell.

Our sense of smell seems to hold some of the strongest memories for us of all the senses; some people report memories flooding back to them after smelling a long-forgotten odor. After the death of a loved one, for example, sometimes the person's smell still on clothing or other personal belonging can be comforting to those left behind. Even though our sense of smell may seem strong at times, we know that a number of animals, including dogs, have a far more acute sense of smell than we humans do and seem to need it for survival.

The odors we smell come from gases which give off molecules into the air which stimulate receptor cells deep inside the nose. There seem to be seven primary odors: floral, camphorlike, musky, peppermintlike, ethereal (like cleaning fluid), pungent (like vinegar), and putrid. These categories correspond to the seven kinds of receptor cells found within the nose, and scientists have found that materials with similar odors seem to have similarly shaped molecules.

Our sense of smell gives us important information, and it has also been associated with worship through incense since very early times. It is even mentioned on a clay tablet found at the Sphinx at Giza dated to 1530 BC. The use of incense continues in many kinds of worship today as a powerful and sensuous reminder of our prayer rising to God, sweet and strong.

RESPONDING:

In his second letter to the Christians at Corinth, Paul talks about his apostolic influence being like that of an odor: " . . . thanks be to God, who in Christ always leads us in triumphal procession, and through us spreads in every place the fragrance that comes from knowing him. For we are the aroma of Christ to God among those who are being saved . . . " (2 Cor 2:14–15)

The image Paul uses here is a powerful one for any Christian or believer: that by living a faithful life the "scent" of what's important to me "wafts its way" toward those around me. Can I think of any ways that the "aroma" of the faith of others around me has had an impact on me? Are there some ways that my example can be a source of "fragrance" for those around me by being kind and hopeful and not criticizing or gossiping about others—or other ways? As Paul reminds us, the source of that "perfume" is not us, but Christ at work within us calling us to deeper faith through the "essence" of one another.

God of the incredible variety of smells we experience, thank you for all those who help those wonderful fragrances happen in our lives, from cooks to florists to those who make candles and incense and perfume. Please bless those who have lost the sense of smell and those who have to work around unpleasant odors. Bless, too, those scientists and researchers who help us learn more about and understand our sense of smell.

Help me to be thankful for my nose and its sensitivity, which comes from you, whenever I smell something. Amen.

For Further Reading

THE FOLLOWING BOOKS MAY help you continue to see the everyday objects around you as holy:

Bender, Sue. *Plain and Simple: A Woman's Journey to the Amish.* New York:Harper & Row, 1989 and *Everyday Sacred: A Woman's Journey Home* New York: HarperSanFrancisco, 1995.

Using simple objects like Amish quilts and begging bowls, Sue Bender encourages us to look again at the everyday stuff of life.

Boyer, Mark G. *Home is a Holy Place: Reflections, Prayers and Meditations Inspired by the Ordinary.* Chicago: ACTA, 1997.

Short reflections on everything from an apron to a zipper.

Norris, Gunilla. *Becoming Bread: Embracing the Spiritual in the Everyday.* Mahwah, NJ: Hidden Spring,
———. *Being Home: A Book of Meditations.* New York: Bell Tower, 1991.
———. *A Mystic Garden: Working with Soil, Attending to Soul.* New York: BlueBridge, 2006.
———. *Simple Ways: Towards the Sacred.* New York: BlueBridge, 2008.

Several breathtaking looks at the sacred that lies right before us, hidden in plain sight, seen in simple meditations.

Rupp, Joyce. *The Cup of Our Life: A Guide for Spiritual Growth.* Notre Dame,IN: Ave Maria Press, 1997.

This wonderful book includes six weeks' worth of meditations on our lives as we pray with a simple cup. This resource can be used individually or in a group.

www.ingramcontent.com/pod-product-compliance
Lightning Source LLC
Chambersburg PA
CBHW050822160426
43192CB00010B/1864